The Fundamentals of Piano Tuning and Maintenance

The Fundamentals of Piano Tuning and Maintenance

Jason Cassel

BLOOMSBURY ACADEMIC
NEW YORK · LONDON · OXFORD · NEW DELHI · SYDNEY

Online resources to accompany this book are available at https://www.bloomsburyonlineresources.com/the-fundamentals-of-piano-tuning-and-maintenance. If you experience any problems, please contact Bloomsbury at: onlineresources@bloomsbury.com

BLOOMSBURY ACADEMIC

Bloomsbury Publishing Inc, 1359 Broadway, New York, NY 10018, USA
Bloomsbury Publishing Plc, 50 Bedford Square, London, WC1B 3DP, UK
Bloomsbury Publishing Ireland, 29 Earlsfort Terrace, Dublin 2, D02 AY28, Ireland

BLOOMSBURY, BLOOMSBURY ACADEMIC and the Diana logo are trademarks of Bloomsbury Publishing Plc

First published in the United States of America 2026

Copyright © Jason Cassel, 2026

For legal purposes the Acknowledgments on p. ix constitute an extension of this copyright page.

Cover design: Sally Rinehart
Cover art by Carol Cole

All images created by author.

All rights reserved. No part of this publication may be: i) reproduced or transmitted in any form, electronic or mechanical, including photocopying, recording or by means of any information storage or retrieval system without prior permission in writing from the publishers; or ii) used or reproduced in any way for the training, development or operation of artificial intelligence (AI) technologies, including generative AI technologies. The rights holders expressly reserve this publication from the text and data mining exception as per Article 4(3) of the Digital Single Market Directive (EU) 2019/790.

Bloomsbury Publishing Inc does not have any control over, or responsibility for, any third-party websites referred to or in this book. All internet addresses given in this book were correct at the time of going to press. The author and publisher regret any inconvenience caused if addresses have changed or sites have ceased to exist, but can accept no responsibility for any such changes.

Library of Congress Cataloging-in-Publication Data
Names: Cassel, Jason author
Title: The Fundamentals of piano tuning and maintenance / Jason Cassel.
Description: New York : Bloomsbury Academic, 2026. | Includes bibliographical references and index.
Identifiers: LCCN 2025035432 (print) | LCCN 2025035433 (ebook) | ISBN 9798216380153 hardback | ISBN 9798216380184 paperback | ISBN 9798216380160 pdf | ISBN 9798216380177 epub
Subjects: LCSH: Piano–Maintenance and repair | Piano–Tuning
Classification: LCC ML652 .C36 2026 (print) | LCC ML652 (ebook) | DDC 786.2/19–dc23/eng/20250731
LC record available at https://lccn.loc.gov/2025035432
LC ebook record available at https://lccn.loc.gov/2025035433

ISBN: HB: 979-8-2163-8015-3
PB: 979-8-2163-8018-4
ePDF: 979-8-2163-8016-0
eBook: 979-8-2163-8017-7

Typeset by Integra Software Services Pvt. Ltd.
Printed and bound in the United States of America

For product safety related questions contact productsafety@bloomsbury.com.

To find out more about our authors and books visit www.bloomsbury.com and sign up for our newsletters.

To Rick Baldassin
For paving the way

Contents

Acknowledgments ix

Introduction 1

Unit 1 – **Removing the Piano Action** 3

Lesson 1 – Types of Uprights 5
Lesson 2 – Removing the Case Parts of an Upright Piano 7
Lesson 3 – Removing the Upright Action 11
Lesson 4 – Types of Grand Pianos 16
Lesson 5 – Removing the Case Parts of a Grand Piano 17
Lesson 6 – Removing the Grand Piano Action 23
Lesson 7 – Deep Cleaning 28
Unit 1 **Exam** 32

Unit 2 – **Tuning** 37

Why Start with Tuning 39
Lesson 8 – Beating 40
Lesson 9 – Finding the Correct Tuning Pin 42
Lesson 10 – Tuning a Unison, Part 1: Click Up 45
Lesson 11 – Tuning a Unison, Part 2: Nudge Down 47
Lesson 12 – Tuning a Unison, Part 3: Refine with the Z-axis 49
Lesson 13 – Developing Good Habits 51
Lesson 14 – Tuning the Center String 54
Lesson 15 – Tuning a Unison, Part 4: Check Stability 57
Lesson 16 – Tips for Tuning in the Bass 59
Lesson 17 – Tips for Tuning in the Treble 60
Lesson 18 – Pitch Raises and Tuning an Entire Piano 62
Unit 2 **Exam** 64

Unit 3 – **Upright Regulation** 65

Lesson 19 – The Upright Keystroke 67
Lesson 20 – Three Adjustments on the Key 70

Lesson 21 – Three Measurements from the Hammer to the Strings 75
Lesson 22 – Upright Aftertouch 79
Unit 3 **Exam** 84

Unit 4 – **Grand Regulation** 89

Lesson 23 – The Grand Keystroke 91
Lesson 24 – Three Adjustments on the Wippen 95
Lesson 25 – Four Measurements from the Hammer to the Strings 102
Lesson 26 – Grand Aftertouch 107
Unit 4 **Exam** 112

Unit 5 – **Voicing** 117

Lesson 27 – Voicing for Evenness 119

Unit 6 – **Repairs** 123

Lesson 28 – Pedal Adjustments 127
Lesson 29 – Clicks 129
Lesson 30 – Buzzes and Rattles 133
Lesson 31 – Squeaks 135
Lesson 32 – Double-Striking Hammers 139
Lesson 33 – Sticky Keys 141
Lesson 34 – Ringing Dampers 144
Lesson 35 – Broken Strings 146

Final Exam 150

Bonus Lesson – Running a Business 158

Conclusion – What's the Next Step? 160
Appendix 1 – A Beginner's Toolkit 162
Appendix 2 – Terminology to Remember 164
Appendix 3 – Regulation Specifications 167
Appendix 4 – Answer Key 169
Index 172
About the Author 174

Acknowledgments

I would first like to recognize Carol Cole, the creator of the artwork featured on the cover of this book. Your work captures the beauty of the piano inside and out. Thank you for lending your talent to this project.

Next, this work would not exist without those who have mentored and inspired me along the way.

I will forever be indebted to Keith Kopp and Jim Busby for taking me under their wings and patiently introducing me to this field.

I am so grateful for Greg Cheng and Bob Parini for always making themselves available to answer my questions without judgment.

I would like to thank Greg Sikora for humbling me by focusing not on my strengths as others had done, but on my weaknesses and how they might be improved.

To Dr. Li Yeoh, thank you for encouraging me to research and write.

To Justin Holcomb, for modeling how to mentor and teach with both passion and compassion.

My deepest gratitude to Rick Baldassin, for seeing in me a lofty potential, then sharing liberally the knowledge and wisdom required to strive for it.

I would also like to recognize my wife Nora and our children, who have supported me every step of our journey together.

Lastly, as a person of faith, it feels appropriate to thank God for guiding me to this fulfilling career and for placing the people listed above in my path.

Introduction

On a scale of 1 to 10, how much do you want to learn how to work on pianos?

For our purposes, let's say that a 1 means "I want to learn just enough to tune my own piano" and a 10 means "I want to make this my full-time career." With a 5 sounding something along the lines of "I see this as a possible side-hustle, or a hobby in retirement."

I work at a university and one of my responsibilities is to mentor students who have expressed a desire to work in our shop. My experience has shown that only around two out of every ten students are committed enough to achieve the level of competency we look for in a potential hire. For the other 80 percent, their initial excitement is quickly swallowed up as the difficulty of learning to tune a piano sets in. Perhaps my favorite exchange took place with a student studying accounting. He'd been coming to practice tuning for a couple of weeks. During one of our mentoring sessions, he stopped halfway through tuning a note, set down the tuning lever and said, "Remind me how much it costs to have a piano tuned." I told him the going rate for our area and he turned to me and said, "I think I will be able to afford that. Thanks again for this opportunity." We shook hands and he left. Sadly, I've never had a music major tell me that.

If you embark on this journey, you will need to invest hundreds of dollars in tools and at least six to nine months of frequent practice. Realistically, this isn't a significant investment of time or resources when considering this is nearly all that is required to break into a new career. All the same, it is more than what many people expect.

So, returning to my question: Where does your interest level fall on a scale of 1 to 10? If it is anything less than a 5, then this book probably isn't for you. You will benefit far more from immersing yourself in my book, *The Piano Owner's Guide: Essentials of Care, Maintenance & Mechanics*.

This is because the amount of time and effort required to learn how to tune a piano exceed the benefits of knowing just enough to service your own instrument. It will take you multiple hours to tune your first piano, and even then, it will probably not be polished or stable enough to meet your musical needs. The real benefits only come later down the road, when tuning times are closer to an hour and the results are more refined; and you'll never get to that point by tuning your own piano once or twice a year.

I know this is an unusual introduction. How many books start by encouraging a portion of readers to stop reading and pick up a different book? Nevertheless, it is important to be honest and clear from the start. Learning how to work on pianos is like learning how to play the piano. It requires practice—*and lots of it*!

Still reading? Then great! I would like to welcome you to the exciting field of piano technology. There is so much to learn, and this book can serve as your introduction. However, reading this book alone will not make you a piano technician. Think of working through this book like enrolling in a class. As such, it will ask things of you beyond just reading. You will need access to an upright and grand piano to practice on. You will also need to invest in some basic tools and work through some hands-on handwork and exams.

I'm sometimes asked if I think piano tuning and repair is a dying art. I don't believe that is the case. During the COVID-19 pandemic, many piano technicians were concerned. Afterall, they provide services in people's homes. To their immense relief and surprise, many found themselves busier than ever before! As it turns out, when the world had more time at home, they found their pianos calling out to them. So no, I do not believe this is a dying art, in part, because I believe that if this craft were to die, then we would lose a part of ourselves.

Tragically, the only thing that does seem to be dying is the opportunity to learn the art of working on pianos. There was a time when many community colleges and trade schools offered certificate programs. A handful of universities even offered degrees. Today, these programs are incredibly rare. I don't have the solution, but I certainly hope that this book will become part of the solution. Primarily, I hope that what you learn from this book can open opportunities for you to gain access to mentorship and education beyond these pages.

Many tuners and rebuilders are open to the idea of taking on a mentee or apprentice; however, they rarely have the time to work with someone with no experience. Beyond that, there is a substantial risk to doing so. How can they be sure that someone has what it takes to stick with it? Because of this, there is a significant difference between a potential mentee that says, "I think I'd like to learn how to work on pianos. Can you teach me?" and another that says, "I already know how to tune clean and stable unisons, and I am familiar with the basic regulation points on upright and grand pianos. I'd like to continue learning under your mentorship, and I'd love to explore ways to help your business grow as we work together."

One of the best ways to find mentorship and education is by joining the Piano Technicians Guild (PTG). Visit www.ptg.org to find your local chapter and information about how you can join. While there is a membership fee, most local chapters welcome visitors free of charge for a limited amount of time. Benefits of joining include local meetings, regional and national conferences and events, a job board, online forum communities, access to educational video content, a subscription to the *Piano Technicians Journal*, and digital access to thousands of journal articles spanning back more than a century—not to mention that most of those articles are stored in a searchable index. PTG also offers the exams required to become a Registered Piano Technician (RPT). You'll notice that this book does not come with a certificate of completion. Instead, I invite you to use the experience you gain from this book to start your journey toward becoming an RPT.

There is a demand for well-trained piano technicians. You might just be what your musical community needs. Reading this book, together with my first book, can serve as the basis for gaining the education required to meet those needs.

***

To get the most out of this book, be sure to watch the video content available at the link below. The videos will be indicated in the text with this symbol ♪.
Link to Video Content and full color images: https://www.bloomsburyonlineresources.com/the-fundamentals-of-piano-tuning-and-maintenance

UNIT 1

Removing the Piano Action

1 Types of Uprights

While most people can tell you the difference between an upright and a grand piano, very few people have any idea that there are different types of upright pianos. Believe it or not, there are four different types. From smallest to largest, they are:

1. Spinet
2. Console
3. Studio
4. Upright grand

If you live in the United Kingdom or Australia, then these terms may not apply as strictly. All the same, it is worth knowing how to identify each type.

Spinet pianos are quite small (Figure 1.1). They usually only come up to about the height of your waist. A quick way to tell is to check to see if the top of the music desk (the piece of wood that holds the sheet music) is higher than the lid of the piano. If so, then it is likely a spinet. (Note: In the UK, the lid is usually referred to as the top.)

These pianos feature what is called a drop action. In this unique design, the back of the key pulls up on a long piece of metal that transmits the key movement to the rest of the action (Figure 1.2). Spinets were incredibly popular during the 1930s and 1940s. Many

Figure 1.1 *Spinet piano. Notice how the music desk is higher than the top of the piano.*

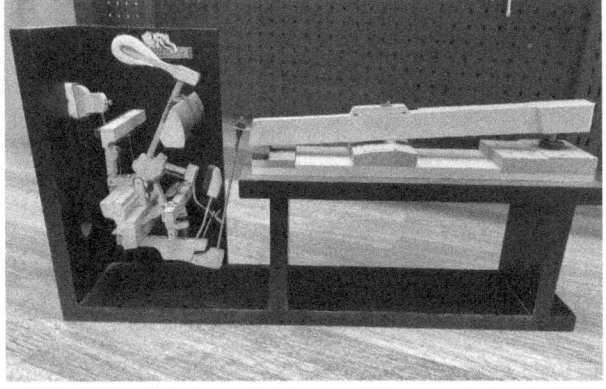

Figure 1.2 *Spinet piano drop action. Notice the piece on the back of the key that drops down to connect to the rest of the action.*

Figure 1.3 *The keys of a console piano. Notice how they slope down.*

Figure 1.4 *Studio upright piano action. Notice that the keys do not slope down.*

of the "grandma's pianos" out there are spinets. These pianos stopped being produced around the late 1980s.

A console piano is a little bit taller than a spinet, but that little bit goes a long way. Instead of a drop action design, the back of the keys of a console upright slope down so that the remainder of the action parts can rest on the back of the keys (Figure 1.3). Otherwise, these pianos function much like a studio.

A studio upright is the standard style and really the only style still in production. These pianos feature straight keys with the remainder of the action parts sitting on the back of the keys (Figure 1.4). For the remainder of this book, when I talk about an upright piano, I will be referring to the studio upright style.

An upright grand is the tallest of all the styles, usually coming up to about your shoulder (Figure 1.5). The name is a little confusing. They have nothing to do with grand pianos. They are just big. The action on these pianos features a long wooden piece called a sticker that connects the back of the key to the rest of the action parts (Figure 1.6). These pianos were incredibly popular around the turn of the twentieth century. They were often adorned with breathtaking casework. Don't let the stunning exteriors deceive you; nearly all these pianos are over one hundred years old.

The procedures laid out in this unit for removing case parts and removing an upright action refer to those of the modern studio upright. The same is true for the unit covering upright regulation. Because of this, you will be best served if you can find a studio upright on which to practice. A console piano would be an acceptable next best option.

Figure 1.5 *Upright grand.*

Figure 1.6 *Upright grand action. Notice the long wooden piece on the back of the key connecting to the rest of the action.*

Hands-on Homework: *Consider the upright pianos in your life. What style do you own? How about your parents? Grandparents? Neighbors? Friends? Find a studio or console upright you can practice on as you work through this book.*

2 Removing the Case Parts of an Upright Piano

Terminology to Remember

Table 2.1 *US and UK terms (differences in bold)*

USA	UK
Lid	**Top**
Top board	**Top door**
Fall board, key cover, or nameboard	**The fall**
Bottom board	**Bottom door**

A quick note on terminology. Different English-speaking countries will use different terms for the various parts of the piano and its action. In the text, I will use the American terminology since that is what I am most familiar with. At the beginning of many lessons, I will include a table like Table 2.1 to provide terminology used in the United Kingdom. If you live in Australia, New Zealand, Canada, or some other English-speaking country, then there is a good chance that you will use either the US or UK terms, however, be sure to work through the list of terminology in the appendix of this book with a local mentor to see what is most commonly used in your region of the world.

Now, onto the lesson!

To service a piano, you must first gain access to the inner workings of the instrument. This requires removing what are called the case parts. In this lesson, I will walk you through how these parts are typically removed on an upright piano.

Opening the Lid

Most upright piano lids can simply be lifted from the front. They are either hinged in the middle or at the back. While most newer pianos are designed so that they can be propped open on their own, the lid on some older pianos will keep rotating away from you and risk bending the hinge. In these pianos, you will need to use a tool called an upright lid prop to hold the lid open while you tune or regulate the piano (Figure 2.1).

Figure 2.1 *Upright lid prop.*

If the lid rests against the wall when opened, then place a microfiber cloth between the lid and the wall to avoid scratching any surfaces.

On some upright pianos, there is a hinge on the bass side (left side), and a lid prop stick attached to the treble side (right side), similar to the way the lid opens on a grand piano (Figure 2.2). In this style, you may need to remove the pin that runs through the hinge to completely remove the lid to service the piano. This pin can be difficult to remove. A good approach is to grab the end of the pin with a set of pliers, then tap the side of the pliers with a hammer (Figure 2.3).

Figure 2.2 *An upright with a built-in lid prop.*

Figure 2.3 *Tapping the pin to remove the lid.*

Removing the Top Board

The top board is the long piece of wood that holds up the sheet music. It is usually connected to the piano by some form of latch located on the back side near the top on each end (Figures 2.4 and 2.5). These latches can be released by rotating them. On some pianos the top board is held in place by screws that attach to the sides of the case. Once the latch has been disengaged, or the screws removed, lift the top board up and pull it toward you to remove it.

Rest the top board somewhere safe where it will not be damaged or

Figure 2.4 *The top board latches.*

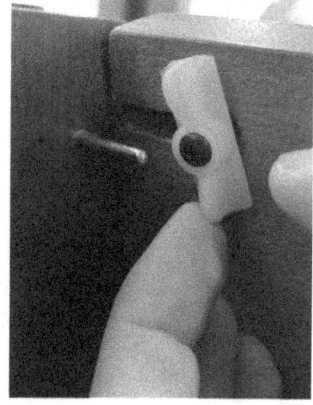

Figure 2.5 *The top board latches.*

knocked over by pets or children. When leaning it against a wall, be sure to place a microfiber cloth between the top board and the wall to avoid scratching any surfaces (Figure 2.6).

Removing the Fallboard

The fallboard is a piece of wood that can be folded down to cover the keys. This piece is also referred to as the "key cover," or the "name board" (since the name of the piano brand is usually included on it).

The fallboard may simply lift out vertically (Figure 2.7), or you might have to remove a screw from each end first. There are other designs out there as well, so examine the parts to discover what needs to be done to detach it. Once it has been removed, place the fallboard somewhere safe.

Figure 2.6 *The top board stored safely.*

Removing the Bottom Board

The final case part to remove is the bottom board (sometimes called the kneeboard). This is a piece of wood underneath the keys, just above the pedals. The most common way to remove it is by pushing up on a spring that holds the board in place, and then pulling the top of the board toward you (Figure 2.8). Sometimes there are two springs, one at each end of the panel. On some pianos, instead of a spring there is a wooden lever that can be rotated one way to lock the bottom board in place and rotated away to allow for its removal (Figure 2.9).

In Video 2.1, I remove all the case parts on an upright piano.

♪ **Video 2.1—Removing the case parts of an upright piano.**

Figure 2.7 *Removing the fallboard.*

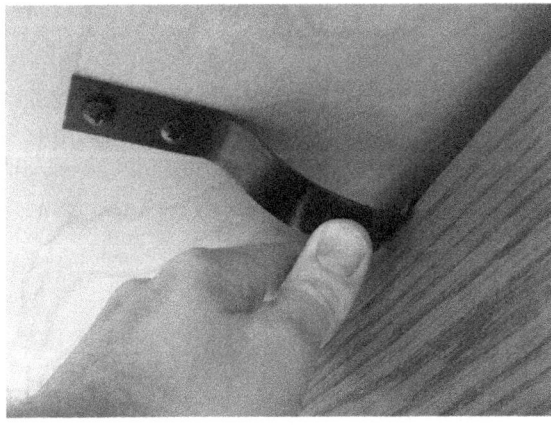

Figure 2.8 *The bottom board spring.*

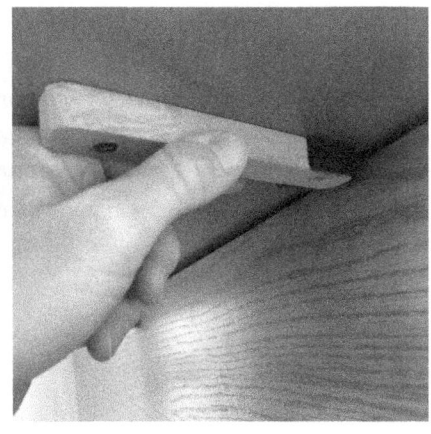

Figure 2.9 *The bottom board lever.*

Some Common Exceptions

Figure 2.10 *One type of Yamaha fallboard removal.*

Figure 2.11 *Baldwin Hamilton. Notice the prop on the bass end of the piano holding up the lid and top board.*

Before we wrap up this lesson, I want to share a couple of common exceptions to the normal set up. Trust me, just when you think you've seen it all, you will find a new case part configuration. Awareness of these more common exceptions will likely come in handy at some point.

First, it is important to know that on some pianos the top board and the fallboard are connected and come off together. Simply rotate the latches holding the top board in place and you can pull both pieces out at the same time. Be careful. This set up can be heavy and awkward to carry.

Second, on certain Yamaha pianos, the fallboard is released by closing it and then lifting the back of it toward you. You can then access the latches on each end that hold it in place (Figure 2.10). This isn't difficult, but it does take a minute to figure out if you haven't come across it before.

Finally, Baldwin Hamilton pianos open in an incredibly unique way. On this model, the lid and the top board are connected. As you lift the top board, the lid rotates up with it. Reach inside the left-hand side of the top board and you will discover a support that can be rotated out and propped on the side of the piano (Figure 2.11). Like I said, just when you think you've seen it all …

Hands-on Homework: *Take this book with you and remove the case parts of your practice upright piano while reading the instructions. It can be helpful to have a friend or mentor present during your first few attempts. Your assignment is to remove the case parts and return them to their proper positions in the piano at least three times before reading the next lesson.*

I know you just can't wait to keep reading, but trust me, taking a few minutes to complete these Hands-on Homework assignments will make a HUGE difference in your retention. We will be covering a lot of material in this book, and it can be tempting to think, "I don't need to stop reading to do that. It seems straightforward enough. I've got this!" Believe me, when you're the one doing it, things get more difficult. So seriously, stop reading and go over to your practice piano and complete this homework assignment before you read on!

3 Removing the Upright Action

Terminology to Remember

Table 3.1 *US and UK terms (differences in bold)*

USA	UK
Key stop rail	Key stop rail
Pedal rods	Pedal rods
Practice pedal rod	**Celeste rail**

Question 3 of *The Piano Owner's Guide* is entitled "How Does the Piano Action Work?" In it, I explain that there are four main components of the piano action, which are the:

1 Key
2 Wippen ("Lever" in the UK)
3 Hammer
4 Damper

In an upright piano, the hammers, wippens, and dampers are attached to rails mounted on a metal bracket that can be removed if needed for repairs and maintenance. We will refer to this simply as "the action" moving forward. The keys remain in the piano when the upright action is removed.

Removing the Keys

Before we discuss how to remove the action, let's first learn how to remove a key. With the case parts removed you will notice one more piece of wood that runs just behind the front section of the keys. This piece is called the key stop rail (Figure 3.1). This rail is generally

Figure 3.1 *The key stop rail.*

attached by screws at each end, and it is not uncommon for an additional screw or nut to be placed near the middle of the keyboard.

With the key stop rail removed you now have access to the keys. They are not connected to the rest of the action. They are held in place by a pin in the middle of the key and another pin underneath the front of the key. To remove a key, simply lift it up evenly with two hands, one at the front and the other somewhere near the back. Do not pry the key up from the front, as this may damage the bottom section of the key that goes onto the pin.

To return the key, use one hand to push the rest of the action parts for that note out of the way. Then with your other hand, align the hole on the bottom of the key with the pin that holds the middle of the key in place. Once the key has been returned, you can gently rest the action parts back onto the back of the key.

Video 3.1 shows the process for removing and returning a key.

Figure 3.2 *A practice pedal rail removal with a screw system.*

♪ **Video 3.1—Removing a key.**

Removing the Upright Action

Now for the exciting part: removing the action. This is tricky, but it is also sure to impress. Fortunately, you don't need to remove the action to tune the piano, but it is required for certain repairs and maintenance. There are a lot of nuances here, so I will be using a step-by-step checklist to help you not miss anything.

Figure 3.3 *A practice pedal rod rail without a screw system. The arrow points to the spring that needs to be disconnected.*

Step 1: If applicable, start by removing the practice pedal rail (sometimes called the "muffler rail"). This is the long felt strip that falls in between the hammers and the strings when the practice pedal is engaged on certain upright pianos. This rail can usually be removed by loosening a screw on the bass side of the system (Figure 3.2). If not, then the metal pieces that hold the practice pedal rod in the sides of the piano can be bent slightly to remove the rod. In this type, a spring on the left-hand side will also need to be disconnected (Figure 3.3).

Step 2: Remove the two to four nuts or screws holding the brackets in place (Figure 3.4). Most of the time you can loosen them with your fingers. Sometimes they are so tight that you might need to use vice grips.

Step 3: Disconnect the pedal rod for the left pedal. This is usually inserted into a hole in a metal piece on the bass side

Figure 3.4 *These nuts hold the action in place.*

(left side) of the long rail on which the hammers rest. Simply pull up on the rail and the rod should fall out (Figure 3.5). Sometimes the dowel isn't connected in any way, it just pushes up on the rail. There is no need to remove this type.

Step 4: Put your left hand on the leftmost bracket. Grab the rail the hammers rest on with your right hand around three-quarters of the way over (Figure 3.6). Make sure you have a firm grip and then pull the action slightly toward you until the brackets clear the bolts that hold the action in place.

Step 5: This is the big moment! Pull the action up slightly and then diagonally up toward you. You can't pull it straight up because then the dampers will bump into the center bolt to which the action was secured (Figure 3.7). Be sure to lift high enough to clear the pedal rod for the left pedal. Finally, as you lift the action out, the pedal rods for the right and middle pedal will fall out and will likely make a loud noise. This is normal, so don't panic!

Figure 3.5 *Disconnecting the pedal rod for the left pedal.*

Step 6: The action is now removed. Set it down gently on a flat surface. The action can usually stand up on its own. However, it should never be left unattended.

Video 3.2 shows the entire action removal process.

🎵 **Video 3.2—Removing the upright action.**

Figure 3.6 *How to hold the upright action when removing it.*

Returning the Upright Action

How do you get the action back in? This is the hardest part. Essentially, you will go through the same process in reverse, but it is *much* easier said than done.

Step 1: Put your left hand on the leftmost bracket. Grab the rail the hammers rest on with your right hand around three-quarters of the way over. Make sure you have a firm grip.

Step 2: Lift up on the action and insert it carefully back into the piano at a slight angle with the top of the action leaning toward you. Remember not to let the dampers hit the bolt in the middle of the piano. You will also need to lift the action high enough to clear the left pedal rod unless you fully removed it earlier.

Figure 3.7 *Watch to be sure you don't bump the dampers on this bolt.*

Step 3: Do not let go of the action until the bottoms of the brackets are properly seated on the supports located near the backs of the keys (Figure 3.8). Once the bottoms of the brackets are in place, you can ease the tops of the brackets back underneath the bolts, but only slightly. You aren't done yet, but you can take a deep breath and let go of the action. Well done!

Step 4: While the previous step is the more precarious, this step is often the most difficult. You must now return the pedal rods to their connection points in the action. If the pedal rods fell completely out, then you will need to remove the bottom board and reinsert them into the bottom of the pedal system (Figure 3.9).

Figure 3.8 *Aligning the bottom of the bracket to the support.*

With the action in place, but not tightened back onto the bolts, you can rock the action front to back as needed to squeeze your hand around the side(s) of the action and reinsert the pedal rods (Figure 3.10). Sometimes, there isn't enough room to squeeze your hand around the side of the action. On these pianos, you will need to guide the pedal rods into place from the bottom.

On some pianos, only one pedal rod needs to be inserted (typically on the bass side). Often, there are two pedal rods on the bass side that need to be reinserted. My least favorite is when there is one rod on the bass side and another on the treble side. This last setup can be particularly frustrating because it always seems like as you try to get the

Figure 3.9 *Reconnecting a pedal rod at the bottom.*

second rod in place, the first one inevitably falls out! In short, be emotionally prepared to not look very cool during this step.

The only tip I can offer is that you can press the pedals to lift a rod you've already inserted slightly to keep it from falling out. For example, if you inserted the pedal rod for the right pedal and are now attempting to insert the pedal rod for the middle pedal, then you can press the right pedal slightly to ensure that the rod for the right pedal doesn't fall out while you insert the rod for the middle pedal.

Figure 3.10 *Reconnecting the pedal rods at the top.*

Step 5: You did it! The hard part is over. Double check that the felts on the dampers are aligned to the strings, then push the action back toward the strings and tighten the bolts or screws that hold it in place.

Step 6: Return the pedal rod for the left pedal if applicable by lifting up on the long piece on which the hammers rest and reinsert the pedal rod.

Step 7: Finally, if applicable, return the practice pedal rod.

Video 3.3 shows the entire process for returning the action.

♪ **Video 3.3—Returning the upright action.**

Hands-on Homework: *Take this book with you and work through the step-by-step procedure for removing keys, removing the action, and returning the action on your practice piano. Have a friend or mentor present during your first few attempts to help you. Your assignment is to remove and return at least three keys and then to remove and return the action at least three times before reading the next lesson.*

4 Types of Grand Pianos

I almost didn't include this lesson because I didn't feel like there was much to say. I then realized that to avoid confusion, it was probably worth taking a moment to clarify things. Unlike upright pianos, the configuration of modern grand pianos is much more standardized and has been for the last one hundred years or so. The only real difference is in their lengths. You'll often hear people say that they have a "baby grand" or a "parlor grand," but there really isn't a hard and fast rule for what those terms mean. The expressions are perhaps best understood as marketing terms, and not as technical definitions.

Even still, grand pianos could be grouped roughly into one of three length categories:

1. Grand pianos under 6 feet long.
    - These pianos make up the majority of the in-home market.
2. Grand pianos between 6 feet and 7 feet long.
    - These are more common in teaching studios, institutions, or in the homes of more serious players.
3. Grand pianos around 9 feet long.
    - These would be considered "concert grands" and are most commonly found in performance venues.

That's about all there is to it. Of course, you will find many other "definitions" out there, but nothing is official. What is most important for our purposes, is that the procedures for removing and regulating the action will apply to most grand pianos you will encounter.

Hands-on Homework: *Find a grand piano to practice on as you work through this book.*

5 Removing the Case Parts of a Grand Piano

Terminology to Remember

Table 5.1 US and UK terms (differences in bold)

USA	UK
Keyslip	Keyslip
Cheekblocks	Cheekblocks
Fallboard	**The fall**
Lid	**Top**

Much of what is presented in this lesson is included in Questions 6 and 7 of *The Piano Owner's Guide*. Those questions laid out a process for removing a pencil from a grand piano, as well as how to properly open the lid. To spare you from having to cross-reference back and forth, I've decided to include many of the same images and text in this lesson.

Before we can begin, we must first familiarize ourselves with some terminology. The fallboard (labeled 1 in Figure 5.1) is the piece of wood that covers the keys of your piano when closed.

On each side of the keyboard are the cheekblocks (labeled 2). Cute, right? Like those blocks are the piano's cheeks and the keys are its teeth. Maybe that's what they were going for, who knows?

Running across the front of the keys is another piece of wood called the keyslip (labeled 3).

And above those three pieces rests the music desk (labeled 4). This is the piece that holds the sheet music.

Stare at Figure 5.1 until these four pieces are ingrained in your memory. I'll be referencing them often as we move through this lesson.

Opening the Lid

To properly open the lid of a grand piano you will first need to ensure that the hinge pins on the side of the piano are in place and haven't fallen out (Figure 5.2). This is important! If the pins for the lid hinges have fallen out, then the piano lid will fall off when you lift it.

Figure 5.1 *Grand piano case parts.*

Figure 5.2 *The lid hinge pin is falling out!*

Next, open the front section of the lid. You are now ready to lift the lid up. Get a good grip and make sure you lift it high enough so that you don't smack the bottom of the lid with the lid prop.

Now for the hard part: what hole does the lid prop go into? This is a common mistake you will see everywhere. The hole closest to the center of the lid is for the full stick. The one closest to the edge of the lid is for the half stick. If that sounds too complicated, then just remember that the lid prop must be perpendicular to the lid. Think 90-degree angle (Figures 5.3 and 5.4).

Removing the Music Desk

The music desk is the piece of wood on which people rest their music. Of all of the case parts, this one tends to be the easiest to remove. Which is convenient, since it is the only piece that needs to be removed to tune the piano since it blocks access to the tuning pins.

In most grand pianos the music desk can be removed by grabbing it securely and simply sliding it toward you. On others, the music desk can be pulled straight up. A more complicated exception is found on some older American-made pianos. In these systems, the music desk can only be pulled up when a pin on the underside of the music desk slides up through a slot on a track attached to the side of the piano (Figure 5.5).

Removing the Case Parts in Common Setup #1

1 Remove the fallboard
2 Remove the cheekblocks
3 Remove the keyslip

This setup is common on many Asian and European-made pianos. First, you need to remove the fallboard. Start by looking at the bottom left and bottom right corners of the fallboard. Do you see any screws? If so, you will need to remove those first.

Once the screws are removed, or if there were no screws in the first place, all you need to do to remove the fallboard is simply stand in the middle of the piano, grab it firmly with both hands and pull it straight up. If your piano follows this setup, then the fallboard should come right out. Gently set the fallboard somewhere safe.

Next you will need to remove the two cheekblocks. Look underneath each one and you will either see a screw, or a wingnut. Remove the screw or wingnut, then lift the cheekblock up and out of the piano. Older pianos may have an additional screw that goes into the top of the cheekblock, but this is less common.

Figure 5.3 *Lid opened incorrectly.*

Figure 5.4 *Lid opened correctly.*

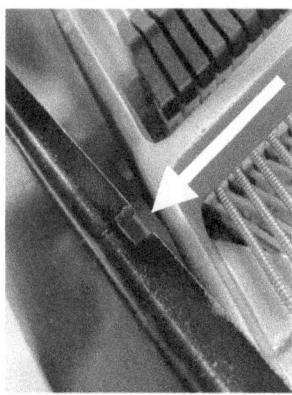

Figure 5.5 *This is the slot that the pin on the bottom of the music desk needs to slide through for it to be removed.*

Figure 5.6 *Slot for the fallboard.*

Finally, you can remove the keyslip. It should come straight out when lifted. Unless it is screwed in place from underneath. In which case, you will need to remove the screws first.

Returning the Case Parts on Common Setup #1

1 Return the keyslip
2 Return the cheekblocks
3 Return the fallboard

To return the case parts in this setup, simply follow this same process in reverse. Start by reinserting the keyslip. Then return the cheekblocks and screw them back into place.

Getting the fallboard back on is a little trickier. Notice the slots on each side of the piano (Figure 5.6). Now locate the pin or rectangular piece on each side of the fallboard (Figure 5.7). Your objective is to insert those pins into the slots. Stand in the center of the piano, hold the fallboard firmly with both hands, and align the pins to the slots the best you can. This will likely mean that a section of the fallboard needs to be slightly inside the piano. Once aligned, lower the fallboard evenly so that the pins go in *at the same time*. That last part is important. If one side falls in first, don't try to be a hero, simply pull it out and start over until they both go in together. Once in place, return the two screws to the bottom right and left sides of the fallboard (if applicable).

Figure 5.7 *This piece is inserted into the slot on the side of the piano.*

Don't worry. It's not as bad as it sounds. Video 5.1 shows the process for removing and returning the case parts for a piano with Setup #1.

🎵 **Video 5.1—Removing and returning the grand piano case parts in Setup #1.**

Removing the Case Parts in Common Setup #2

1. Remove the keyslip
2. Remove the fallboard and cheekblocks together

This setup is more common on certain American-made pianos. It is slightly trickier than Setup #1, but not terribly difficult with some practice.

In this setup, the fallboard is attached to the two cheekblocks. To remove the fallboard, you will need to remove the keyslip, then the fallboard and cheekblocks at the same time. Let's work through this step by step. Some pianos may follow a slightly different process than the one described here. This procedure is the most common.

Step 1: Remove the keyslip. On some pianos, the keyslip can be pulled straight up to remove it. On others, you will need to remove a few screws from under the piano first.

Step 2: Unscrew the cheekblock screws.

Step 3: Stand in the middle of the piano. Grab the fallboard firmly with your hands and pull straight up slightly. This should remove both the fallboard and the cheekblocks together.

Step 4: Gently rest the fallboard on the front of the sharp keys.

Step 5: Lift up slightly on one side of the fallboard, then carefully remove the cheekblock from that side (Figure 5.8). Rest the fallboard on the front of the sharp keys again.

Figure 5.8 *Removing the cheekblock.*

Step 6: Lift up slightly on the other side of the fallboard and carefully remove that cheekblock.

Step 7: You can now remove the fallboard and set it somewhere safe.

Returning the Case Parts in Common Setup #2

1. Return the fallboard and cheekblocks together
2. Return the keyslip

To put things back together:

Step 1: Start by resting the fallboard on the front of the sharp keys.

Step 2: Lift up each side of the fallboard and reattach the cheekblocks to the pins on the sides of the fallboard.

Step 3: Stand in the middle of the piano. Grab the fallboard firmly with your hands and lift the fallboard straight up slightly. Don't lift too high as the cheekblocks might fall off.

Step 4: Slowly navigate the fallboard and cheekblocks back into the piano. You may need to guide the fallboard up and over a spring on the inside of the piano before it will fall into place (Figure 5.9).

Step 5: Once in place, reinstall the cheekblock screws and the keyslip.

Once again, if that sounded scary, then watch the video. It's almost as bad as it sounds, but not quite. Video 5.2 shows the process for removing the case parts from a grand piano with Setup #2.

♪ **Video 5.2—Removing and returning the grand piano case parts in Setup #2.**

Hands-on Homework: *Determine if the case parts on your practice grand piano are configured in Setup #1 or Setup #2. Then carefully remove and return the case parts at least three times before continuing.*

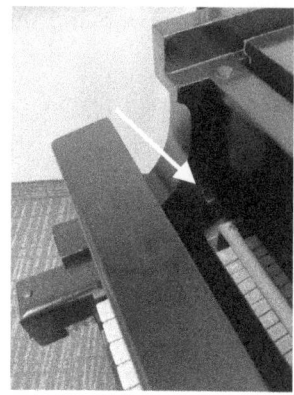

Figure 5.9 *You will need to lift the fallboard over this spring.*

6 Removing the Grand Piano Action

Terminology to Remember

Table 6.1 *US and UK terms*

USA	UK
Action stack	Action stack
Key stop rail	Key stop rail
Sostenuto monkey	Sostenuto monkey

Pulling the Action

Now that we've learned how to remove the case parts, we can discuss how to remove the grand piano action.

With the case parts removed, you can now pull the action out of the piano and rest the front of the keys on your lap. To do this, you will grab the action on either end of the keyboard. As you do so, *ensure that you are not pressing any keys*. Some common locations to grab are the pins of the sides of the action, the metal bracket that the hammers are attached to, the ledge next to each end of the key stop rail (Figure 6.1), or the brass bolts that come up near the middle of the keys (Figure 6.2).

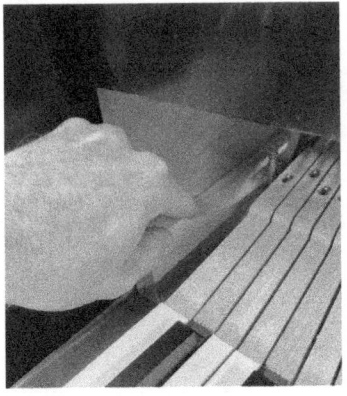

Figure 6.1 *Grab here to make sure you aren't depressing any keys.*

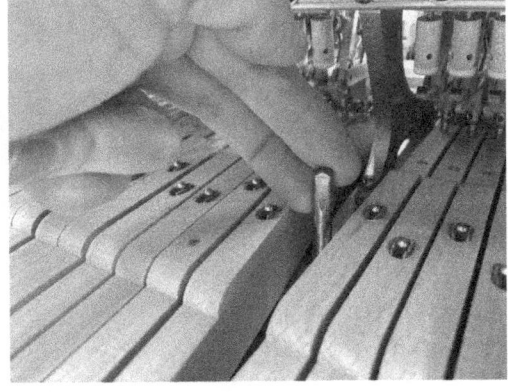

Figure 6.2 *Grab here to make sure you aren't depressing any keys.*

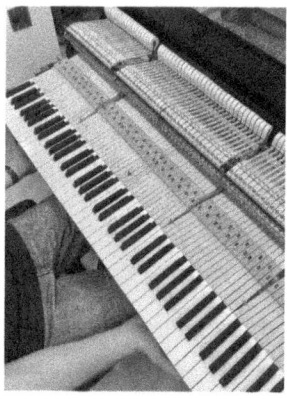

Figure 6.3 *Grand piano action with the front of the keys on my lap and the back of the keys resting on the piano.*

Once you have a secure grip on any of these locations, slowly pull the action toward you. Do not, I repeat, DO NOT press any key. Doing so will cause the hammer to rise. When you pull the action out, that hammer will break as it collides with the inside of the piano. Be especially careful with the bottom and top notes of the piano. Have a friend or mentor spot you during your first few attempts. I know it sounds crazy, but you can be utterly convinced that you aren't pressing down a key, only to have your spotter shout "Careful!" Looking down you will find you *were*, in fact, slightly depressing the top note of the piano! Even experienced technicians break hammers in this way.

When the action is pulled most of the way out of the piano, you will be able to place your hands underneath the keys and grab onto the underside of the frame and slide it the rest of the way out. You should be able to balance the front of the keys on your lap, while the back of keys rest on the front of the piano (Figure 6.3).

In an upright piano, the keys stayed behind when the action was removed. In a grand piano, the dampers stay behind. If you need to access the damper system, then you will need to completely remove the action and set it somewhere safe. If the piano bench is padded, then you can balance the action on top of the bench (Figure 6.4). If the bench is not padded, first protect the finish with a moving blanket before setting the action down on the bench.

To lift the action, you will need to grab it securely with your hands on either end, or with one hand supporting the end of the action and your other hand holding onto one of the metal brackets of the action stack (Figure 6.5). The action is not only heavy but also incredibly awkward to carry. Whenever possible, move an action with two people.

Video 6.1 covers how to remove the grand piano action.

🎵 **Video 6.1—How to remove the grand piano action.**

Figure 6.4 *A grand action balanced on a padded bench.*

Figure 6.5 *Carrying a grand piano action.*

Removing a Key

To remove the keys on a grand piano, you must first remove the key stop rail. Just like on an upright piano, this is a piece of wood that runs just behind the front section of the keys (Figure 6.6). This rail is generally attached by screws at each end, with additional nuts in the middle.

Figure 6.6 *The key stop rail.*

Next, you will need to remove the action stack. This is the metal bracket to which the hammers and wippens are attached. The action stack is held in place by screws on the front and back of the bracket (Figure 6.7). Remove the screws and place them somewhere where they won't get lost. It is a good idea to arrange the screws in order so that the screws return to the holes they were in originally.

Remove the action stack screws in the following order:

1 Screws that go in at a diagonal (if applicable)
2 The end screws
3 Any remaining screws in the middle

Figure 6.7 *Action stack screws.*

You are almost there! On nearly all pianos, once the screws are removed, you can simply lift up the action stack to remove it. On most New York Steinways, however, there is a bonus piece that needs to be detached. This piece has a delightful name, the "sostenuto monkey." No, I am not making that up!

This piece is located on the back side of the action in between the bass hammers and hammers for the midrange of the piano. It can be detached by inserting a screwdriver underneath the spring that holds it in place, prying the spring up, and swinging the monkey free of the spring (Figure 6.8).

You can now lift up the action stack to remove it. Place it somewhere safe. Once the stack is removed, you finally have access to the keys. To remove a key, simply lift it up evenly with two hands, one at the front and the other somewhere near the back. Do not pry the key up from the front, as this may damage the bottom section of the key that goes onto the pin.

Figure 6.8 *Disengaging the sostenuto monkey.*

Once you are finished servicing the keys, you can return the action stack. Make sure all the holes are aligned, then reinsert the action stack screws in reverse order:

1 Middle screws

2 End screws

3 Any screws that go in at a diagonal (if applicable)

While some of you might already know this, there is an important life lesson to learn here. Namely, before you tighten a screw, turn the screw to the left (counterclockwise) until you feel it fall into place. Then turn the screw to the right (clockwise) to tighten it. This prevents cross threading and ensures that the screw will go back into the hole in the same way every time. Finally, be sure to return the sostenuto monkey under its spring, if applicable.

Video 6.2 demonstrates how to remove the action stack and a key.

♪ **Video 6.2—How to remove the action stack and a key on a grand piano.**

Returning the Grand Piano Action

To return the action to the piano, start by resting the back of the keys on the front edge of the piano. Then slowly start to push the action back into the piano. As you do so, make sure that the treble side (right-hand side) of the action doesn't jam up into the shift pedal return spring. This spring is attached to the inside of the piano on the treble side (Figure 6.9).

Figure 6.9 *Make sure the action makes it around the spring inside the piano.*

Once the action has cleared the return spring, lift up slightly on the front of the keys and continue to push the action back into the piano (Figure 6.10). Once the bolts in the middle of the piano have cleared the front of the case (see the arrow in Figure 6.10), you can stop lifting up slightly and push the action all the way back into the piano. You will likely feel some resistance from the shift pedal spring. This is completely normal. Just push through it.

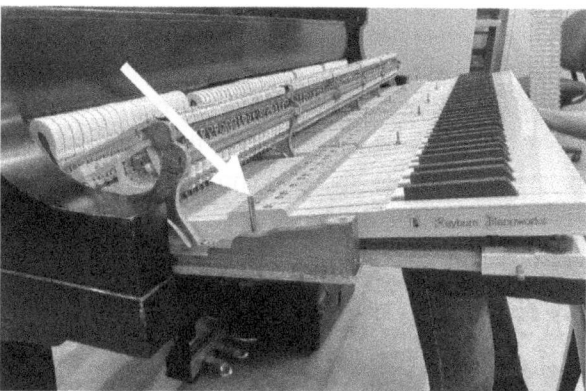

Figure 6.10 *Notice that I am lifting up on the front of the action slightly until the bolts indicated by the arrow clear the front of the case.*

On most pianos, the action will be correctly located when it is pushed in as far as possible. On other pianos—Steinways in particular—the action is properly positioned by the cheekblocks. In other words, you will need to first insert the cheekblocks for the keys and hammers to be in their proper position.

Once the action is in place, you can return the case parts as described in the previous lesson. Video 6.3 shows how to return the grand piano action.

🎵 **Video 6.3—Returning the grand piano action.**

Hands-on Homework: *Remove the case parts and then have a friend or mentor watch you as you carefully* pull out the grand piano action and rest the front of the keys on your lap. Then return the action. Repeat this process at least three times before continuing.

7 Deep Cleaning

Tools You Will Need (Figure 7.1):

- Black paint marker
- Can of compressed air
- Microfiber cloths
- Paintbrush
- Portable vacuum
- Screwdriver (flathead and Phillips)
- Soundboard cleaners
- Windex

Figure 7.1 *Tools needed for deep cleaning a piano.*

Deep Cleaning an Upright Piano

Upright pianos are fairly easy to clean since they are mostly covered by the case parts. One area that does tend to build up a lot of dust is the area behind the bottom board. Use your vacuum to clean up the dust in this area and you'll have a customer for life (Figure 7.2).

You can do the same for the back of the piano if you can reasonably pull it far enough away from the wall. Be careful not to scratch the floor when moving the piano.

Figure 7.2 *Vacuuming behind the bottom board.*

Another area that can be cleaned is underneath the keys. Remove the case parts and then remove all the keys and gently set them down in order. With the keys removed you can vacuum up the dust (Figure 7.3). WARNING: Beware of rat or mouse droppings and nests. If an upright piano is left for a long time without being played, then rodents can move in. The area under the keys is like a luxury suite! If you find evidence of rodents, stop cleaning, and put on gloves and a mask immediately. Be sure to use a vacuum with an HEPA (high-efficiency particular arresting) filter. Airborne fecal matter is a health risk as well.

Figure 7.3 *Dust underneath the keys.*

Finally, before you put the keys back on, you can clean the tops and the sides of the keys. Use Windex sprayed on a microfiber cloth to wipe down the sides of the natural keys (Figure 7.4). Use a black paint marker to touch up the sides of the sharps (Figure 7.5).

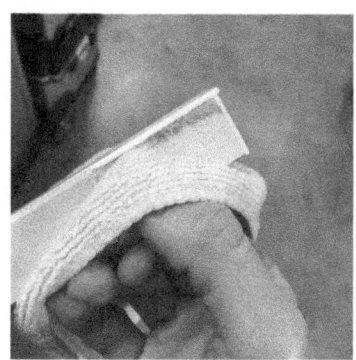

Figure 7.4 *Cleaning natural keys.*

Figure 7.5 *Cleaning sharp keys.*

Deep Cleaning a Grand Piano

Figure 7.6 *Cleaning the soundboard.*

In Question 9 of *The Piano Owner's Guide* I suggested some user-friendly options for cleaning a grand piano. These included using a can of compressed air to blow out the dust from under the strings and around the tuning pins. Sometimes dust is caked on so thick that even compressed air isn't enough. In these cases, the only way to really get the dust off the soundboard is to use a set of soundboard cleaners. These tools are designed to slide in between the strings. They are inserted parallel to the strings, then rotated. The tool can then be run up and down the soundboard to clean off the dust (Figure 7.6). Vacuum the tool off when the dust builds up. Then insert the tool in a new section and repeat the process. They even sell a small one for the very top of the piano and an extra-long one to reach underneath the bass strings. The before and after results are sure to impress (Figures 7.7 and 7.8)!

Figure 7.7 *A soundboard before deep cleaning.*

Figure 7.8 *A soundboard after deep cleaning.*

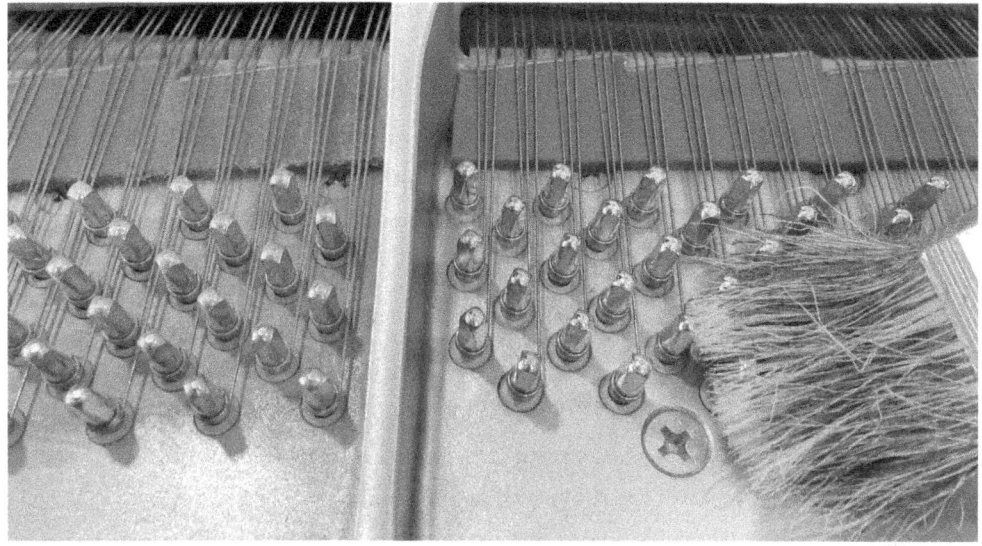

Figure 7.9 *Cleaning around the tuning pins. The area on the left has not been cleaned. The area on the right has been cleaned. Full color images can be found in the following link: https://www.bloomsburyonlineresources.com/the-fundamentals-of-piano-tuning-and-maintenance*

To clean around the tuning pins, you can use a paintbrush in one hand to kick up the dust and a vacuum in the other hand to suck up as much of the dust as possible as you go (Figure 7.9).

You can also pull out the action and set it on the piano bench. Use a can of compressed air to clean it. Then vacuum out the inside of the piano while the action is removed.

Finally, if you remove the action stack, then you can clean and touch up the sides of the keys as well.

Hands-on Homework: *Clean your project upright and grand.*

Unit 1 Exam

You did it! You made it through Unit 1. In some ways, it feels like we've only just scratched the surface. I suppose that's because we have. On the other hand, we are already a quarter of the way through this book! Familiarizing yourself with the case parts and actions assemblies of both upright and grand pianos is fundamental to everything that follows, especially for the units on regulation and repair.

Hopefully you aren't just reading through this book but are actually taking the time to complete the Hands-on Homework assignments. It is impossible to learn how to work on pianos from a book. You have to actually get out there and do it! Find a local mentor to guide you and your chances of success will skyrocket.

Before we continue, we need to make sure that you have retained as much information from this first unit as possible. To help with this, I have created a Unit Exam. The answers can be found in the answer key at the back of this book.

Terminology from Unit 1

USA	UK (differences in bold)
Action stack	Action stack
Bottom board, or kneeboard	**Bottom door**
Cheekblock	Cheekblock
Damper	Damper
Fall board, key cover, or nameboard	**The fall**
Hammer	Hammer
Key	Key
Keyslip	Keyslip
Key stop rail	Key stop rail
Lid	**Top**
Practice pedal rod	**Celeste rail**

USA	UK (differences in bold)
Sostenuto monkey	Sostenuto monkey
Top board	**Top door**
Wippen	**Lever**

Unit 1 Exam

1. True or False:

   The instructions included in this unit for removing an upright action will work on all four types of uprights.

2. True or False:

   The instructions included in this unit for removing a grand piano action will work on nearly all grand pianos.

3. Put the four types of uprights into the correct order from smallest to largest.

4. True or False:

   Spinet pianos are still being manufactured today.

5. True or False:

   Upright grand pianos are still being manufactured today.

6. Which type of upright has keys that slant down at the back?

   a Spinet

   b Console

   c Studio

   d Upright Grand

7. Which type of upright is tall and has a sticker to connect the back of the key to the rest of the action?

   a Spinet

   b Console

   c Studio

   d Upright Grand

8. Which type of upright has a drop action?

   a Spinet

   b Console

   c Studio

   d Upright Grand

9 What size grand piano is known as a "baby grand"?

  a Under 5 feet

  b Under 6 feet

  c Under 6.5 feet

  d There is no formal definition

10 Which of the following are NOT one of the four main components of the piano action? Select all that apply:

  a Hammer

  b Key

  c Jack

  d Backcheck

  e Wippen

  f Damper

11 When opening the lid of a grand piano you should …

  a make sure the lid hinge pins are not falling out;

  b open the front flap of the lid;

  c insert the lid prop at a 90-degree angle to the lid; or

  d all of the above

12 True or False:

  When removing an upright action, the dampers should contact the bolt that held the action in place.

13 True or False:

  The pedal rods will fall out of an upright action when it is removed.

14 When removing an upright piano action, which of the following action components stays inside the piano?

  a Dampers

  b Wippens

  c Keys

  d Hammers

15 When removing a grand piano action, which of the following action components stays inside the piano?

  a Dampers

  b Wippens

  c Keys

  d Hammers

16 True or False:

You should not press a key when removing a grand piano action.

17 When returning the action stack, screws that go in at a diagonal should be inserted …

　a　First;

　b　Last; or

　c　Whenever (the order doesn't matter)

18 True or False:

It is important to turn a screw to the left before you tighten it.

19 True or False:

When returning a grand action, you should lift up the front of the keyboard slightly until the bolts in the middle of the keyboard clear the front of the piano.

20 True or False:

The best way to clean dust from the soundboard of a grand piano is with a vacuum.

UNIT 2

Tuning

Tools You Will Need

Tools to Buy:

- Felt mute
- Papp's mute (optional)
- Rubber mute with handle
- Temperament strip (also called a strip mute)
- Tuning device or piano tuning app (not pictured)
- Tuning lever (not a gooseneck lever)

A Few Notes on Tools

Many of the tools listed above can be found commercially online. Some online schools sell premade tool kits. I've done some work with Piano Technician Academy and their basic tool kit should provide most of what you need as you work through this book.

At some point, you will also want to set up an account with a piano industry supply house. Ask a mentor or search for a supply house online, then fill out an application. Tell them you are reading this book and need their support to set up an account.

Piano tuning levers come in a variety of designs and price ranges. The better the tuning lever, the easier it is to use, which means the easier it is to tune. If you are serious, then you will eventually want to spend a little more money and get a nicer lever. When you are first starting, you can get by with a student lever, just be sure to avoid what is called a "gooseneck lever." These levers are made entirely of one piece that curves from the shaft of the lever to the head (see the bottom lever in the figure below). You want to make sure your lever has at least two pieces: a shaft and a head (see the top lever in the figure below).

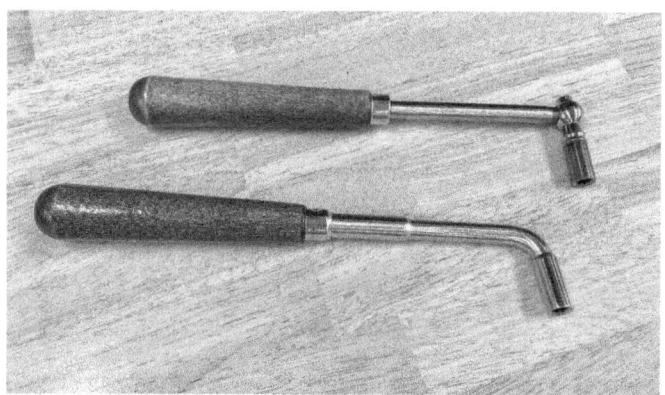

While there are a number of differently sized tuning tips and angles available, a size 2 tuning tip with a 15-degree angle is an excellent option that should work on nearly all pianos.

There are lots of ways to tune a piano. I do not profess to teach the definitive "best way." While I prefer rubber mutes with handles for upright pianos and felt mutes for grand pianos, plenty of well-respected technicians have different preferences. For example, I don't personally use a Papp's mute, but that doesn't mean it isn't worth trying it out for yourself to see if you like it! Many technicians prefer it, especially in the high treble of upright pianos.

Tuning devices and piano tuning apps continue to be improved, and if you are familiar with how to use them, then they all can produce professional-level results. They range in price from a few hundred dollars to over a thousand dollars. Find one that works for you at this moment in your education. Some even offer free trials. Just be sure that you are using a piano tuning app, and not a normal tuning app. I explain why that is in Question 8 of *The Piano Owner's Guide*. Look for the section header "Why a Guitar Tuner Won't Work."

An electronic tuning device is the most expensive tool you will purchase as you work through this book. You won't need it until Lesson 14, so feel free to wait before making the investment if you want to test the waters first before deciding if tuning is for you.

Why Start with Tuning

Coming off the excitement of Unit 1, you may be thinking, "I just learned how to pull the action out of a piano, and I can't wait to dive in!" I can't blame you for feeling this way. In general, people are more captivated by how the piano action works than they are with tuning. When I pull an action for the first time at someone's home, I am often peppered with questions and find myself featured as the subject of an impromptu musical photo op. When I tune the piano, however, most people are more than happy to leave me alone.

That said, tuning is what most piano technicians spend the majority of their time doing. Sure, there are a small handful who work exclusively as rebuilders, and there are even a number of field technicians who have built up a reputation for a specialty in action work. But you shouldn't bank on making a career in this industry without tuning the majority of the time, especially at first. It is therefore worth knowing right off the bat if you have an aptitude for it, and perhaps even more important, if you actually enjoy doing it.

For some, tuning is a fascinating sound puzzle. For others, it is a migraine waiting to happen. There's really no way to know until you get your feet wet. While Question 8 of *The Piano Owner's Guide* presented some of the foundational theory of piano tuning, these lessons will focus on the practical skills you need.

Some of these lessons will be shorter to help break up the nuance of this complicated process into smaller building blocks. Take your time and don't rush through this unit. The shorter lessons may give you a false sense of confidence. You will discover, however, that while you may be able to read through a given lesson in a few minutes, the content within it will likely take hours of practice to internalize.

Are you ready? Let's begin!

8 Beating

When learning how to tune a piano, you are fighting two battles at once. The first is "Can you hear it?" and the second is "Can you fix it?" There is actually a third battle as well: "Can you make it stay?" but we will save that battle for another time.

In my experience, nearly everyone struggles with at least one of these two battles. Many beginners have an excellent ear but struggle to control the tuning lever; while others can manipulate the lever but aren't sure where to stop. If you find yourself in either of these two camps, know that this is completely normal.

If you play music, then you can remember what it was like the first time you picked up your instrument. Did it sound good? Probably not. Did you quit? No! You stuck with it, and with practice you got better. The same is true for learning how to tune a piano. It will take months of practice before you gain the listening skills and control you need to tune accurately, quickly, and with stability.

In this first lesson, we will focus entirely on Battle #1: "Can you hear it?" This doesn't mean that this battle is won after you finish this lesson. You will continue to fight this battle as you work through the lessons that follow, but it is worth taking a moment to develop your ears before you ever touch a tuning lever.

This book will focus on teaching you how to tune a unison. For much of the piano, the hammers strike more than one string. We call the strings that make up a single note a unison. To be in tune, all of the strings in a unison must vibrate in sync with one another. If they don't, then they produce a phenomenon we call beating. This is heard as a "Wah, Wah, Wah, Wah" in the sound. When the strings vibrate in phase with each other, the beating disappears. The closer in pitch the two strings are to one another, the slower the beating. The farther away (sharp or flat) the two strings are from each other, the faster the beating.

Video 8.1 shows a unison with one of the strings out of sync with the other two. Can you hear the beating? As the unison is tuned, can you hear the beating decrease and eventually stop?

♪ **Video 8.1—Beating in a unison.**

While there are many ways to approach learning how to tune a piano, I believe that starting by tuning a unison is the most straightforward. This allows you to focus on listening to beats and controlling the tuning lever without the added complications that accompany aural tuning theory and techniques. Learning to tune a solid and stable unison lays an excellent foundation.

Just don't forget to build on that foundation once it is in place. We will talk more about how to do that in the conclusion of this book.

The Hands-on Homework for this lesson is actually more of an ears-on experience. I have created a tuning quiz in which the strings of different unisons are played. These unisons have three strings: left, center, and right. For now, we will assume that the center string is in the correct place (whether or not that is true). I will use a mute to stop the vibration of either the left string or the right string.

When the right string is muted, we are comparing the sound of the left string to the center string (Figure 8.1). Do these two strings sound like they are in tune with each other? This would mean that they sound like one string being played. We call this "pure," meaning, without beats. Or is the left string out of tune when compared to the center string? This would mean that there is beating when the two strings are played.

When the left string is muted, we are comparing the sound of the right string to the center string (Figure 8.2). How does the right string sound? Is it in tune (pure) or out of tune (beating) when played with the center string?

Hands-on Homework: *Take the audio quizzes online at https://www.bloomsburyonlineresources.com/the-fundamentals-of-piano-tuning-and-maintenance. Determine whether it is the left string or the right string that is out of tune. There is an easy, medium, and hard version of this quiz. Don't move onto the next lesson until you can at least pass the medium level quiz at 100 percent. The answers for this quiz can be found in the answer key at the end of this book.*

Figure 8.1 *Notice the location of the mute. The right string is muted. The left and center strings are free to vibrate.*

Figure 8.2 *Notice the location of the mute. Now the left string is muted, and the right and center strings are free to vibrate.*

9 Finding the Correct Tuning Pin

Figure 9.1 *Tuning pin positions on an upright piano.*

Figure 9.2 *Tuning pin positions on a grand piano.*

Now that we know what we are listening for, we can move onto Battle #2: "Can you fix it?" Let's continue to assume that the center string is correct. Once you've determined which string needs to be moved (the left, the right, or both) you will then need to put the tuning lever on the correct tuning pin (wrest pin in the UK). Each string has its own tuning pin. The pattern for both uprights and grands from top to bottom is: left, center, right (Figures 9.1 and 9.2). Each note has its own set of tuning pins corresponding to the strings of each unison.

Before we continue, we need to talk about the note names.

The lowest C on the keyboard is C1. The next C is C2. The next C is C3. Middle C is C4, and the pattern continues until you reach the C at the very top of the piano, which is C8. Any note that falls between those Cs gets the same number as the C below it. For example, the E above C2 is E2, and the A above C4 is A4.

The notes below C1, are labeled with a zero: A0, A#0 and B0. To a piano tuner, every black key is referred to as a sharp (yes, even D# and A#). Figure 9.3 shows this system laid out on a keyboard.

Let's say you are tuning the unison for E4. You mute the right string to listen to the left string and the center string. You don't hear any beating. You then mute the left string to listen to the right string and the center string. This time, you do hear a beat. You now must put your tuning lever on the bottom pin for this unison. Remember that the layout vertically from top to bottom is left string, center string, right string. If you feel lost, then you

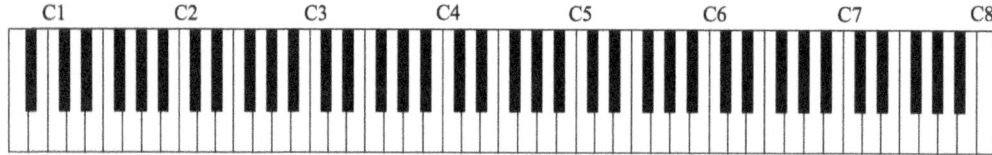

Figure 9.3 *Note numbers on a keyboard.*

can hold down the key for E4 so that the hammer is raised closer to the strings. This can help you locate which set of tuning pins corresponds to E4.

Once you locate the correct pin, you now have to determine the position of your tuning lever. A good rule of thumb is to position the tuning lever as parallel to the strings as possible (Figures 9.4, 9.5, 9.6, and 9.7). This position typically provides you with the most control over the tuning lever.

On a grand piano, following this rule of thumb means that the tuning lever will be facing away from you. Most tuners stand or sit at a slight angle when tuning a grand piano so that they can reach the lever more ergonomically (Figure 9.8).

When tuning a studio or upright grand, I typically stand while tuning. When tuning a console or spinet, I sit on the bench. When tuning a grand piano, I usually stand, however, many tuners prefer to tune sitting down. Find what feels most comfortable for you. Listen to your body. Tuning shouldn't hurt. If it does, then adjust your position.

Now that the tuning lever is on the correct tuning pin, you are ready to start! But first, some Hands-on Homework.

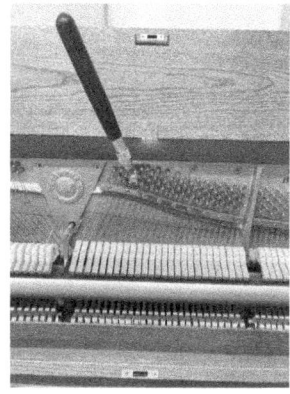

Figure 9.4 *An acceptable position for those who tune with their left hand on the tuning lever. I tune uprights right-handed, but plenty of technicians chose to tune uprights left-handed (even the right-handed ones). There are some ergonomic benefits to this approach if you want to try it out.*

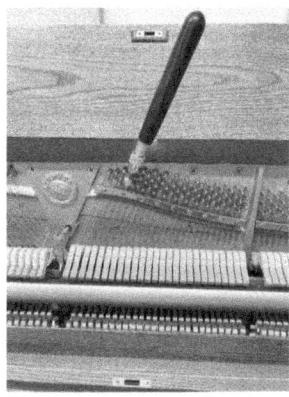

Figure 9.5 *The best position for those who tune with their right hand on the tuning lever.*

Figure 9.6 *Not the best option.*

Figure 9.7 *The worst possible option.*

Figure 9.8 *How to sit when tuning a grand piano.*

Hands-on Homework: *Place your tuning lever on the following tuning pins:*

- *The left string of C4*
- *The right string of A#7*
- *The center string of F5*
- *The left string of D#6*
- *The right string of D#6*

For bonus points, find these same tuning pins on an upright and a grand piano!

10 Tuning a Unison, Part 1: Click Up

A tuning pin is about as long as your pinkie finger. This means that the part you can see is only about a third of the entire length of the tuning pin. The other two-thirds are inside the wood of the pinblock (wrest plank in the UK), which on most pianos is hidden underneath the cast-iron plate (Figure 10.1).

Try this. Grab the end of your pinkie finger and twist it slightly. Then release your finger and observe what happens. The moment you release the pressure you applied, the end of your finger returns to its at-rest position.

The same is true for the tuning pins in the piano. If you only bend the exposed section of the tuning pin, then when you let go, it will likely spring back to its original position. You need to move the bottom of the pin in the pinblock to make the movement stable. The ability to feel when the bottom of the pin moves is at the core of learning how to tune a piano with accuracy and control.

Figure 10.1 *A cutaway view of a pinblock. Notice how much of the tuning pin is in the wood compared to how much is above the wood.*

The Hands-on Homework assignment in this lesson is designed to help you feel when the bottom of the pin moves in the pinblock. The procedure is explained below.

Pick a unison in the middle of the piano. Insert your mute on the right side of the unison to prevent the right string from vibrating. Place your tuning lever on the tuning pin for the left string of this unison. Put your hand on the tuning lever in a thumbs down position, as shown in Figures 10.2 and 10.3.

Now for the tricky part. As you play and hold the note, apply

Figure 10.2 *How to hold the tuning lever for Part 1 on an upright piano.*

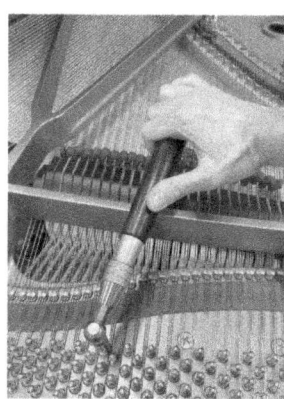

Figure 10.3 *How to hold the tuning lever for Part 1 on a grand piano.*

a small amount of pressure to the tuning lever, pulling it to your right. Do not overdo it. Apply just enough to feel the resistance build up. You should not hear any difference in the sound of the unison. Yes, your goal is to apply pressure *without* hearing any difference in the sound. Play the note every few seconds to make sure the sound doesn't decay too much.

If you do move the pin and hear a difference, then simply try again. If the pitch moves significantly sharp, then you will want to lower it by gently pushing the lever to the left before you try this exercise again. Keep practicing this until you can successfully apply pressure to the lever *without* feeling the pin move.

Once you think you have a sense of how much pressure is required to *not move the tuning pin*, then you can apply just a little extra pressure and feel the pin move. This sensation feels like a click. Sometimes you might even hear a clicking sound, although this is not necessary.

This process is painfully difficult to express in words. Watch Video 10.1 to see how this procedure works in practice.

♪ **Video 10.1—Tuning a Unison, Part 1: Clicking up.**

Hands-on Homework: *Place your mute on the right string of a unison and your tuning lever on the tuning pin of the left string of that unison. Apply just enough pressure to the lever to feel the resistance in the pin, but* do not *move the pin. Hold that pressure for five seconds, then apply just a little extra pressure until you feel the pin "click up" and just barely move. Strive to make the pin move the smallest amount possible. Repeat this process as many times as needed until you start to feel comfortable.*

11 Tuning a Unison, Part 2: Nudge Down

You now know what it feels like when the bottom of the tuning pin moves in the pinblock. Pianos tend to go flat, so if we assume that the left string is flatter than the center string, then as you push through that resistance and "click up," one of two things will happen. Either you will click up into place and the unison will sound pure and lovely. If this is the case, and the bottom of the pin did in fact move, then consider yourself lucky and move onto the next string.

More often than not, the string will click up past the target and be just a little sharper than the center string. When this happens, you need to nudge the pitch back down.

On an upright piano, I like to switch the position of my hand on the tuning lever to hold the top of the lever as shown in Figure 11.1. On a grand piano, I tend to leave my hand in the thumbs down position. Again, listen to your body and select a position that feels natural for you.

There is usually a little slop in the tuning lever. Before nudging down, I first move the tuning lever as far to the left as I can until I feel it start to apply pressure to the tuning pin. I then nudge the lever gently to move the pin as little as possible. There is a significant risk of "banana peeling" and having the pin slip very flat in one big jump. If this happens, simply click the pin back up and start again.

To avoid "banana peeling," I like to think of this nudging movement like waking up someone you love from a nap; not like you might wake up your younger sibling. It is a gentle and loving nudge. If done successfully, you will feel the pin move down ever so slightly and hear the pitch change in small increments. Remember, as you get closer to the target, the beats will slow down. If you hear the beats speeding up, then you know that you have gone too far and need to click up again.

See Video 11.1 to watch this process.

♪ **Video 11.1—Tuning a Unison, Part 2: Nudging down.**

Hands-on Homework: *Place your mute on the right string of a unison and your tuning lever on the tuning pin of the left*

Figure 11.1 *How to hold the tuning lever for Part 2 on an upright piano.*

string of that unison. Nudge the pitch down in the smallest increments you can manage. If you hear the beating speed up, then click up until you are just over the target. Nudge the pitch down again and do your best to stop as close to the target as possible. Repeat this process as many times as needed until you start to feel comfortable, and you no longer experience "banana peeling."

12 Tuning a Unison, Part 3: Refine with the Z-axis

Up until this point, we have thought of moving the tuning lever in a two-dimensional plane. Move the tuning lever to the right and the pitch goes up. Move it to the left and the pitch goes down. But this is only one axis of movement. Let's call it the x-axis (see the black arrows in Figure 12.1). We could also move the tuning lever forward and backward in the y-axis. This is called "flag polling." While some tuners intentionally use this dimension as they tune, I prefer to use the z-axis and move the tuning lever diagonally to refine and hone things in once I know I am close to the target (see the white arrows in Figure 12.1).

Combining everything we've learned so far, the entire unison tuning process looks something this:

Figure 12.1 *The three-dimensional plane of motion for the tuning lever.*

1. Click up until you are just barely above the target.
2. Nudge down until you are very close to the target.
3. Refine with the z-axis until the unison is in tune.

Please note that you can't just jump in and start moving the tuning lever at a diagonal. You must move the pin at the bottom first by clicking up. Then if needed, nudge down until you are just above the target. Only when you are more than 90 percent of the way there can you refine the placement by moving the tuning lever at a diagonal.

If you watch an experienced tuner, you will likely see them make small adjustments to the tuning lever before finishing each string. Those small adjustments tend to be made in the y- or z-axis.

These motions are even smaller than the already small movements we were striving for when clicking up and nudging down. I usually use only my fingers or palm when refining within the z-axis (Figures 12.2 and 12.3).

Figure 12.2 *How to move the tuning lever when refining with the z-axis a grand piano.*

Video 12.1 shows the refining process.

🎵 **Video 12.1—Part 3: Refine with the z-axis.**

Figure 12.3 How to move the tuning lever when refining with the z-axis on an upright piano.

Hands-on Homework: *Place your mute on the right string of a unison and your tuning lever on the left string of that unison. Click the tuning pin up in small increments until you are just above the target. Nudge the pitch down until you are 90–95 percent of the way there. Then try to refine the pitch until it's right on target by moving the tuning lever in the z-axis. Repeat this process as many times as needed until you start to feel like you have a reasonable amount of control over each step.*

Once you feel comfortable moving the tuning pin on the left string, then move the mute to stop the left string from ringing. Repeat this tuning process on the right string. Finally, remove the mute and listen to all three strings of the unison. Does the entire unison sound in tune? If not, can you find the string that is out? It might be that the left string is slightly sharp while the right string is slightly flat (or vice versa). When this happens, the outer strings tend to sound acceptable when compared with the center string, but sound less acceptable when all three strings of the unison are played together.

To complete this assignment, tune the right and left strings of at least five unisons.

13 Developing Good Habits

You did it! You tuned your first few unisons! This is how you will spend around two-thirds of your time when tuning an entire piano. Because of this, getting to a point where tuning unisons feels second nature is absolutely critical. This means (you guessed it) *lots and lots* of practice. Before you spend hours practicing, it is important to make sure you are developing good habits. The following are some of the most common habits that I find myself emphasizing with beginner tuners.

Use Two Fingers

Figure 13.1 *Using two fingers to strike the note when tuning.*

It feels so natural to play the key with one finger when you are tuning, especially if you play the piano. This works great for a handful of unisons, maybe even for an entire piano. But if you go on to do this professionally, then you will thank me for telling you now that if you only use one finger, then that finger will hurt. The solution: use two fingers (Figure 13.1). It doesn't really matter which two. Just pick whatever feels natural.

Don't Move the Lever When You Aren't Playing the Note

This one should be obvious, and yet, I continue to see beginner tuners do this. They play the note. Stop playing the note. Make an adjustment with the tuning lever. Then play the note again. You can't hear the changes you are making unless you are listening to the note while you make them.

Video 13.1 shows me doing this incorrectly and then doing it correctly.

🎵 **Video 13.1—Don't move the lever when you aren't playing the note.**

Don't Tune into the Decay

The best time to listen to the beats in a unison is right at the beginning. The longer the note decays, the less obvious the beats will be. Many beginners have a hard time hearing the beating at first, so they listen well into the decay hoping that their ears will eventually lock onto the beats.

Remember the two great battles. While we've focused our attention on manipulating the tuning lever for the last few lessons, the importance of developing your ear has been ever present. I challenge you to spend most of your time making adjustments as soon as you hear the note being played, not while the sound decays. I know it can be tempting. It can even give you the illusion that you are getting closer to the target; when all that is really happening is that the beats are becoming less obvious as the sound dies off. So, play the note often (around once per second in the middle of the piano). Certainly, every time you feel the tuning pin move, you'll want to play the note again to get a fresh reading.

Once again, Video 13.2 shows me doing this incorrectly and then doing it correctly.

♪ **Video 13.2—Don't tune into the decay.**

Take the Stairs, Not the Slide

I often see people who think they can be faster by ignoring the three steps I presented in Lesson 12 and simply moving the tuning lever right and left until the beats stop. While it is true that these people usually end up at something close to "in-tune." They tend to move the pin more than necessary and their movement lacks control, and thus, the note likely lacks stability. I call this approach "taking the slide" because the pitch slides around until eventually coming to a stop.

I advocate for a "taking the stairs" approach. By clicking the pin up in small increments, nudging down in small increments, and refining with even smaller lever movements within the z-axis, the tuner is in control throughout the process and the pin is much more likely to be stable.

Let me show you what I mean. Video 13.3 shows me doing this incorrectly and then doing it correctly.

♪ **Video 13.3—Take the stairs, not the slide.**

Give Yourself the Opportunity to Get Off the Ride

Finally, don't be afraid to take your hand off the tuning lever. So many beginners waste time by arriving at the target only to keep pushing and pass it. As you nudge the tuning pin down, be sure to stop and listen. Take your hand off the tuning lever if needed. Give yourself an opportunity to get off the ride.

As is so often the case, the video demonstration in Video 13.4 is likely more helpful than the text above.

♪ **Video 13.4—Give yourself the opportunity to get off the ride.**

Hands-on Homework: *Detune the outside strings of each note for one octave in the center of the piano. Then tune the unisons (left and right strings) until they are all pure and beatless. Repeat this exercise until you can complete it in under twenty minutes. This will take hours of practice to accomplish. Come to terms with that now before you begin so you don't get discouraged. Do not move* on until you can accomplish this task within the twenty-minute time limit. If possible, don't move on until you have a mentor check and approve of your work.

This assignment can be an excellent time to stop and reevaluate your interest. As you practice, pay attention to how you feel about practicing. Does the challenge draw you in? Or does the mere idea of picking up the tuning lever fill you with dread? Let this assignment serve as a filter to tell you whether your interest is strong enough to push through the countless practice hours that lie before you. There's no shame in setting down this book and saying, "Now I never have to wonder if a career as a piano tuner was for me." That discovery is well worth the time and energy you've invested to reach this point.

14 Tuning the Center String

Figure 14.1 *Inserting a strip mute.*

As mentioned, I believe that the last Hands-on Homework assignment is one of the best assessments for determining if piano tuning is for you. If you finished the last Hands-on Homework assignment (and I mean truly finished it—especially if a mentor signed off on your work), then there is a high probability that you have what it takes to tune an entire piano. Which is where we will turn our attention in the lessons that follow.

The next step on your journey is to tune the center string. Up to this point, we have assumed that the placement of the center string has been correct and focused our attention on tuning the left and right strings to the center string as a clean unison. This results in individual notes that sound in tune with themselves, but if the center strings are not in the correct place, then the intervals in the piano will not sound in tune (no matter how beatless the unisons are).

To isolate the center strings, you will need to insert a temperament strip (also called a strip mute). This is usually a red piece of felt that is inserted in between each unison to mute the left and right strings. To insert a temperament strip, first press on the right pedal to lift all the dampers (we don't want to pinch the damper felts as we insert the mute). Then use a flathead screwdriver to push a section of the mute in between the strings of two unisons. Then pinch the mute, pull up a small section, and insert your screwdriver again (Figure 14.1). Repeat this process throughout the midrange of the piano. This can be tricky the first couple of times you do it. Watching Video 14.1 will help.

🎵 **Video 14.1—Inserting a strip mute.**

Now that the outside strings are muted, how do we know where to set the center strings? There are two methods. The first is the classic approach used for centuries: using a tuning fork and your ears to aurally set a temperament octave, then expanding that tuning throughout the keyboard. Needless to say, this process is complex and deserves its own book. This doesn't mean that it is not worth learning. In fact, I think that at some point, every piano tuner should learn how to tune a piano completely by ear. We will discuss resources for learning aural skills in the conclusion of this book.

The second method is much more straightforward to a beginner. It is to use an electronic tuning device. This is a piano tuning device, not a violin or guitar tuning app. At this writing, most of the options available are app-based, but some physical tuners are still available. Some apps offer student discounts or monthly subscriptions. Shop around and ask a mentor which device they would recommend.

Once you've selected a tuning device, read the owner's manual to determine how that specific device measures what the tuning should be for each piano. This is a critical step. You cannot simply turn on the device and start tuning. Each piano is unique and will require a custom tuning. Often, the device will have you measure a handful of notes so that it can create a custom tuning for that piano. Read the manual to determine what your device requires.

Once you have measured the piano, then you can use the visual interface to tune the center string for each note. Make sure the note you are tuning matches the note on the screen. Some devices have lights or moving bars to stop, others have a spinning dial. While each interface has a learning curve, all modern tuning devices can produce professional-level results when the procedures for using them are followed properly.

As you experiment with your own device, take the opportunity to focus on your technique with the tuning lever. Having a visual reference to help you see how far you are moving the string can be a great aid in helping you make smaller pin movements, leading to increased stability and control.

Hands-on Homework: *Practice inserting the strip mute at least three times. Then, before moving forward, put in the practice hours needed to achieve the following goal:*

Tune the center strings in an octave in the midrange of your practice piano to your tuning device. Then tune the outside strings to the center strings. Repeat this assignment until you can tune all three strings for each note within that octave in under thirty minutes. As you tune the outside strings, you can either remove the strip mute entirely and use a rubber or felt mute to isolate each string, or you can remove the strip mute one string at a time as you go.

How do you make this assignment repeatable? Afterall, once you finish, that octave is now in tune. Does this mean that you will need to knock out the tuning on each string before you can work through the assignment again? You could, but an easier approach might be to simply offset your tuning device. Let me explain.

Most tuning devices default to tuning A4 to 440 Hertz. Piano tuners use "cents" to measure the distance between notes, with 100 cents in each half step.

To tune A4 to 441 Hertz, you could offset your tuning device up 4 cents. Doing this would mean that the notes you tuned before are now slightly flat from the new target. This allows you to tune the center strings to your tuning device again without having to detune them. Once all the center strings are tuned to the device. The right and left strings of each unison will be slightly flat when compared to the center string. Allowing you to tune the unisons again as well.

Once you finish, that octave is now in tune. This time with A4 tuned to 441 Hertz.

To practice again, simply tune the octave with your device set to A440.

Alternating between tuning the octave up and down 4 cents, allows you to practice tuning the same octave over and over again without the need to detune the strings each time.

Check the operation manual for your tuning device to learn how to offset your device up and down.

15 Tuning a Unison, Part 4: Check Stability

You might think that this lesson is out of order. Shouldn't Part 4 come after Part 3? Well, from a technical perspective, yes; but from an emotional perspective, I've found that it is much better to leave this final piece of the tuning process until this moment. This is because, when you are first learning to tune a unison, it is a triumph to get it sounding in tune. To an absolute beginner, nothing is more discouraging than hearing that all of their hard work was in vain because the note wasn't stable.

You are no longer a beginner. You can tune an entire octave in less than thirty minutes! That means that you can handle this final step in your unison tuning journey. In truth, this is the final battle. The first battle is "Can you hear it?" The second battle is "Can you fix it?" and the final battle is "Can you make it stay?"

You already know everything you need to know to tune a stable unison. Ensuring that the bottom of the pin clicks up and moving the tuning pin as little as possible are among the two best things you can do. The question is, "How do you know if your unison is stable?" The answer is by using what is called a test blow.

A test blow is an intentional firm blow intended to see whether the strings will hold when struck with force. Simply tune a unison as you have been up to this point, then before moving forward, give it a nice firm blow with two fingers. It shouldn't hurt your fingers or your ears, but it should be harder than your normal tuning volume. After the test blow, listen to the unison again to see if any of the strings have slipped.

Generally, a "best two out of three rule" will work. If the unison slipped, mute the left string, and listen to the center and right strings. If the center and right strings sound in tune, then you know that it is the left string that has slipped. If the beating continues, then mute the right string to listen to the center and left strings. If the beating stops, then you know that it is the right string that has slipped.

If the beating sounds the same when you mute the left string and the right string, then that means that the center string is the one that has slipped.

This is more difficult to describe than it is to watch. Video 15.1 shows how this works.

♪ **Video 15.1—Test blows and the "best two out of three rule."**

Hands-on Homework: *Don't move forward until you can tune two octaves in the middle of the piano, all three strings, checking for stability (fixing any strings that slip) in under thirty minutes. Yes, this is double the number of strings from the last assignment, in the same amount of time. Time to put in some serious practice hours! There are only three lessons on tuning left. So don't rush past this homework assignment. You will need the foundation you build as you work toward this goal to take on the challenges presented in the bass and treble.*

16   Tips for Tuning in the Bass

Now that you are familiar with the basics of tuning technique, it is time to branch out into other areas of the piano. Tuning in the bass is not harder than tuning in the middle of the piano, but it is different. First, the bottom notes only have one string. With a tuning device, these are fairly straightforward. Which is great, because the bottom notes are some of the hardest to lock in when tuning with your ears. Soon, there will be two strings per note. This is called the bi-chord section. I typically insert my mute on the right string to tune the left string to the device. I then remove my mute and tune the right string to the left string as a unison.

After tuning the left string to the device, you can move your mute over two strings so that it is muting the right string of the next note, that way you are ready to keep tuning. This also helps you not lose your place.

When you reach the top of the bass section, you often can't place your mute on the right string of the last note. On the last two notes, I tune the left string of the second to last note to my device, then tune the right string of the last note to the device. I then remove the mute and tune the other sides as a unison. That was awkward to read. This process is illustrated in Video 16.1.

🎵 **Video 16.1—Tuning the top two strings in the bass section.**

The hardest part about tuning in the bass is that the bass strings excite a lot of overtones, or partials as they are called in piano tuning. These partials can make it difficult to tell when things fall into place. Often, beginner tuners will tell me that the note isn't in tune because they can still hear something happening in the higher partials. My advice is for them to knock the note out of tune and identify the loudest "ugliest" beat. I then tell them to lock their ears onto that offensive beat and to stop when it goes away (Video 16.2). Once it is gone, then they will just have to live with any other noise that they hear in the unison. Moving the tuning pin up or down will only reintroduce the most offensive beat back into the sound. Once they come to terms with this, they usually do just fine.

🎵 **Video 16.2—Removing the most offensive beat.**

Hands-on Homework: *Don't move forward until you can tune the entire bass and midrange in less than an hour. Remember that you don't need to knock out the tuning of each string before you practice. Simply alternate between tuning the piano at A440 and A441 by offsetting your tuning device. This process was explained in the instructions after the Hands-on Homework in Lesson 14.*

17 Tips for Tuning in the Treble

You are now ready to take on the most difficult section of the piano. The treble is hard to tune for several reasons. First, the sound decays so fast that the useful information in the sound quickly dies off. Second, the strings are shorter, meaning that a five-minute turn of the tuning pin will have a greater effect on the pitch than it did in the bass and midrange. This means that not only are things harder to hear but also that the tuning lever is harder to control.

How do you overcome these challenges? Start by hitting the key more often. Seriously, by the time I am tuning the top octave or so, I am basically hitting the key non-stop.

Another reason why tuning in the treble is more difficult is that the beats are often incredibly fast. Instead of thinking about slowing down the beat rate, I think about cleaning up the sound. When the note is out of tune, it sounds "crunchy" and "messy." When it is in tune, the clarity returns. Hitting the note often will help you determine when that moment happens.

While it is still important for the bottom of the tuning pin to move in the pinblock, I tend to jerk the tuning lever more often when tuning in the treble. This seems to help with control.

This next difficulty is unique to upright pianos. As you leave the midrange and make your way into the treble, you can no longer comfortably place a strip mute in between the strings. This is particularly true for the last few notes with dampers. There just isn't much room left. I believe this is why the treble is where many people seem to really love using a Papp's mute. Now would be a great time to try yours out if you haven't already. As for me, I usually insert my rubber mute between the center and right strings just above the damper (Figure 17.1). I then tune the left string to the tuning device, then tune the other two strings to the left string. In fact, I actually prefer to do this throughout the entire piano. This allows me to tune using only one mute. I don't recommend this to beginners when they start tuning in the midrange, but you are no longer at square zero. So, try this out in the treble, then experiment with it in the midrange.

When tuning the high treble of a grand, I prefer to stand on the treble side of the piano (Figure 17.2).

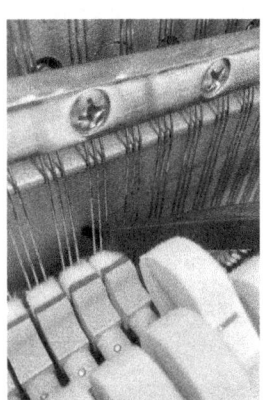

Figure 17.1 *Where to insert the mute in the treble of upright pianos.*

Figure 17.2 *Standing on the side of a grand piano to tune the treble.*

One final difficulty is what are called "false beats." These can occur anywhere in the piano but tend to be more common in the treble. A false beat is when a string is beating with itself. If you suspect a false beat, then you can mute the other two strings and play the note while listening to each string individually. If you hear a beat rate when only one string is sounding, then you've found a false beat (Video 17.1).

🎵 **Video 17.1—A false beat.**

What do you do when you encounter a false beat? The best advice I can offer you is to identify the string with the false beat in it and tune it last. Meaning that if the false beat is in the left string, then I would tune the right string to the tuning device, then tune the center string to the right string, and finally move the left string up and down until it is in the best location possible. When all else fails, remember that while false beats are absolutely infuriating to tuners, most pianists have no idea they even exist. They are just part of the piano's unique sound. Just do the best you can.

Video 17.2 shows me tuning in the treble. Notice the differences in my tuning lever technique and in how often I play the key.

🎵 **Video 17.2—Tuning in the treble.**

Hands-on Homework: *Do not move forward until you can successfully tune the entire treble in less than an hour.*

18 Pitch Raises and Tuning an Entire Piano

Having completed the previous homework assignments, you can now tune the entire bass and midrange in less than an hour. You can also tune the entire treble in less than an hour. This means that in theory, you can tune an entire piano in under 2 hours! This is no small accomplishment. You know firsthand how much work is required to get to this point. Very few who embark on this journey ever make it this far.

Before you attempt to tune an entire piano, we must first discuss the concept of pitch raises. I touched on these briefly in *The Piano Owner's Guide*, but here is a refresher. We can use a tuning device to measure how flat or sharp a piano is in cents, with 100 cents in each half step.

Over the course of a year or so, a piano tends to fall around 1–15 cents flat. Within this range, the piano strings can be pulled up to pitch without much issue. Once a piano is over 15–20 cents flat, then the piano will likely need to be tuned twice. The first tuning is called a pitch raise. The goal of this first pass is to simply raise the pitch of the piano to be closer to the target. Only then can you hope to tune the piano with any level of accuracy.

Most tuning devices come with pitch raise functions that will do the math for you, but as a general rule, you need to pull the pitch 25 percent sharper than how flat it is. Meaning that if a note is 20 cents flat, then you will need to pull it 5 cents sharper than the actual target for it to land close to the desired pitch. If the note is 40 cents flat, then you'd need to pull it 10 cents sharp of the target pitch. If the note is 16 cents flat, then you'd need to pull it 4 cents sharp, and so on.

Pianos don't go flat by the same amount in each range, so when doing a pitch raise you (or your tuning device program) need to generate a game plan. Let's say you measure all of the "A"s on your piano. Table 18.1 provides an example game plan for the overpull you might use. Again, your tuning device will likely do this for you.

Table 18.1 *Possible overpull game plan*

Note	A1	A2	A3	A4	A5	A6	A7
How Flat is the Note?	4 Cents	4 Cents	20 Cents	20 Cents	30 Cents	40 Cents	50 Cents
How Much Overpull is Needed?	1 Cents	1 Cents	5 Cents	5 Cents	7.5 Cents	10 Cents	12.5 Cents

Don't be too fussy. It is important to remember that the goal of a pitch raise pass is not accuracy. You know you'll be tuning the piano again. So just get the strings close to the target and don't worry if the unisons are completely beatless or stable. Speed is the objective during this first pass.

In extreme cases, such as pianos that are 80–100 cents flat, I wouldn't overpull more than 10–15 cents, no matter what the math dictates.

By now, you've already tuned each area of your practice piano a handful of times. So, if it originally needed a pitch raise, then you likely already worked through that process without realizing it. That said, being aware of pitch raises will prove critical as you venture out into the real world. Often the first pianos you will be asked to tune will have been neglected for some time.

That's it!

After countless hours of practicing, you are now finally ready to tune an entire piano from start to finish.

Before you jump in, Video 18.1 shows me tuning an entire piano. Not the most exciting watch mind you, but I'm surprised by how often people request this. Enjoy, and good luck!

♪ **Video 18.1—Tuning an entire piano.**

Hands-on Homework: *Tune an entire piano in less than two hours. Tune your piano as many times as needed to fit within this time limit.*

Unit 2 Exam

Congratulations! If you made it this far, then you are serious. Experience shows that roughly 20 percent of those who set out to learn how to tune have the discipline to stick with it. As you now know firsthand, tuning is hard—much harder than most people think.

Take a well-deserved victory lap, but also realize that your journey is far from over. Most professionals can tune a piano in under an hour. Which means that, you need to be twice as fast as you are now! To make a living as a full-time tuner, you will need to be able to tune four to five pianos per day.

In my experience, the magic number seems to be somewhere around 100 pianos. Yes, you read that right. Once you've tuned 100 pianos, then you are *starting* to get the hang of things.

Additionally, while you can technically tune an entire piano, you really only know how to do one thing: tune unisons. Learning to tune by ear is a critical skill that will push you and build upon the listening skills and tuning technique you have developed. As mentioned previously, we will discuss resources for learning aural skills in the conclusion of this book.

Finally, it doesn't matter how clean your unisons are if you don't know how to fix a sticky key or address other routine repairs. I am surprised by how often I get a call from someone who says, "I want a technician, not just a tuner. My last guy didn't know how to fix these issues. They only knew how to tune!"

This is why we will turn our attention to regulation and repair for the remainder of this book.

What's that? Oh right, your Unit 2 exam! I nearly forgot. The exam for this unit is to reach out to a family member or close family friend and offer to tune their piano for free. There is something about tuning a real piano in the real world that adds a certain level of nervousness that practicing can never truly capture. Brace yourself for a pitch raise. Put everything you've learned in this unit to the test and make notes of any non-tuning related issues you encounter. Who knows, you might just be able to return to address them as you continue to learn.

UNIT 3

Upright Regulation

Tools You Will Need

Tools to Buy:

- Combination handle
- Capstan regulator
- Square capstan screw wrench
- Let-off regulator
- 8-inch tweezers
- Millimeter ruler with slide
- Small pieces of felt
- Balance rail punchings
- Front rail punchings

A Few Notes on This Unit

Pianos have hundreds of moving parts. Honestly, it can feel a little overwhelming. Realizing that it's essentially just the same thing eighty-eight times can help the piano action feel more approachable. With that in mind, this unit does not seek to guide you through an entire regulation procedure. Instead, it focuses on familiarizing you with the points of regulation on a single note. The same is true for the next unit on grand regulation. While this certainly doesn't stop you from regulating these points on each note of your practice piano, it is important that you realize that certain critical regulation steps will not be covered in this book. For example, we will not be covering the process for leveling, squaring, and aligning the keys of your piano.

I will be using millimeters for all the regulation measurements throughout this book. The adjustments we are making are small. While plenty of technicians use inches in the United States, I personally find it much easier to visualize the difference between 10 millimeters and 10.5 millimeters, than it is to visualize the difference between 0.40 inches and 0.41 inches.

Finally, I want to emphasize again that the regulation steps in this unit refer to the action of a modern studio upright. They can also be applied to most console pianos. However, we will not be discussing spinets or upright grand pianos.

19 The Upright Keystroke

Terminology to Remember

Table 19.1 US and UK terms (differences in bold)

USA	UK
Key	Key
Wippen	**Lever**
Damper	Damper
Hammer	Hammer
Capstan	Capstan
Damper spoon	Damper spoon
Jack	Jack
Hammer butt	Hammer butt
Let-off button	**Set-off button**
Backcheck	**Check**
Catcher	**Balance hammer**

The upright piano action has four main components. These are:

1. The key (which is pressed by the player).
2. The hammer (which strikes the strings).
3. The damper (which dampens the strings).
4. The wippen (which connects the key movement to the hammer and damper).

There are three main contact points between the action parts (Figure 19.1):

1. The capstan (on the key) contacts the wippen.
2. The jack (on the wippen) contacts the hammer butt.
3. The damper spoon (on the wippen) contacts the damper lever.

Let's take a closer look at each of these components and how they interact.

The key is a simple lever. You press the front of the key down, and the back of the key moves up. The back of the key contains a wooden or brass piece called a capstan. This piece communicates the key movement to the wippen. This contact point is labeled 1 in Figure 19.1.

As the capstan moves the wippen, the jack contacts the hammer butt and starts to move the hammer toward the strings. This contact point is labeled 2 in Figure 19.1.

When the hammer is about halfway to the strings, the damper spoon (attached to the wippen) engages the damper lever, which causes the damper to be lifted off the strings. This contact point is labeled 3 in Figure 19.1.

Just before the hammer strikes the strings, the toe of the jack contacts what is called the let-off button (Figure 19.2). This causes the jack to swing out from under the hammer butt. This moment is called escapement. The hammer is now propelled the last few millimeters toward the strings (Video 19.1).

🎵 **Video 19.1—Escapement in an upright piano.**

After the hammer hits the strings, it rebounds and is caught by the backcheck (which is also attached to the wippen). The part of the hammer assembly that contacts the backcheck is called the catcher. As long as the key is held down, the catcher will remain in contact with the

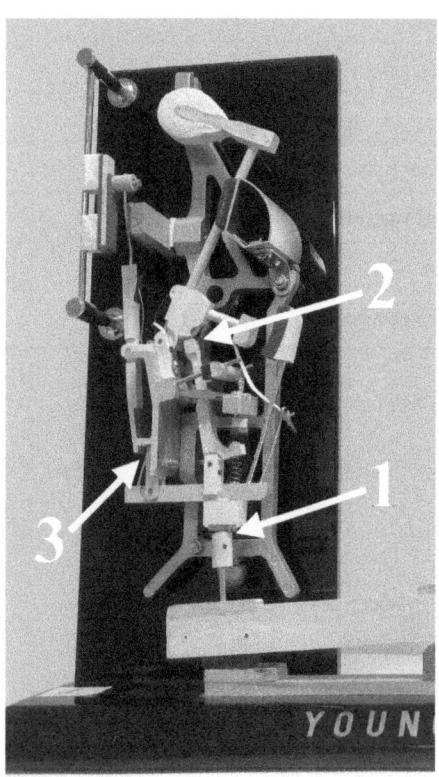

Figure 19.1 *The upright action contact points.*

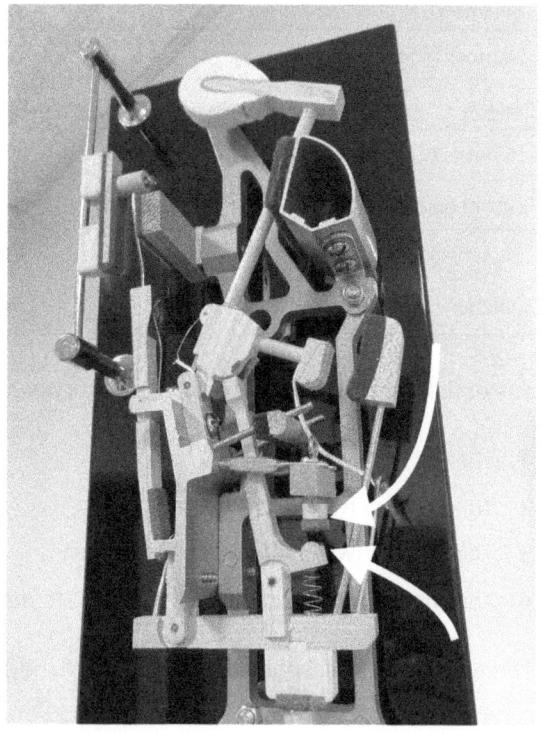

Figure 19.2 *How escapement works on an upright piano. The bottom arrow points at the jack toe. The top arrow points at the let-off button. When those two pieces touch, it starts to move the jack out from underneath the hammer assembly.*

backcheck. Technicians refer to this position as the hammer being "in check" (see Figure 19.3).

When the key is released, the jack returns under the hammer butt so that the key can be played again. The damper then contacts the strings to dampen the note. Finally, the hammer and key return to their rest positions.

If this lesson felt rushed, then reread Question 3 of *The Piano Owner's Guide* and come back and read through this lesson again.

Hands-on Homework: *Remove the case parts of your upright practice piano. Play a note slowly and observe the action parts in motion. Make note of each step in Table 19.2 as you see it take place. Note that you will not be able to see the damper spoons with the action in the piano.*

After making your observations, take out a piece of paper and try to write out the upright keystroke steps from memory. Don't move on until you can list them all in the correct order.

Figure 19.3 *The hammer is "in check." Meaning that the note has been played, the key is being held down, and the catcher is in contact with the backcheck. This holds the hammer closer to the strings.*

Table 19.2 *The upright keystroke step by step*

Step 1: The player presses a key.
Step 2: The capstan starts to lift the wippen causing the jack to contact the hammer butt, moving the hammer toward the string.
Step 3: When the hammer is about halfway to the string, the spoon (on the wippen) starts to lift the damper off the strings.
Step 4: The jack toe contacts the let-off button causing the jack to no longer contact the hammer butt.
Step 5: The hammer strikes the strings!
Step 6: The hammer rebounds and is caught by the backcheck (on the wippen).
Step 7: The key is released by the player.
Step 8: The jack and damper start to return to their at-rest positions.
Step 9: The jack returns to its position under the hammer assembly ready to play the next note if needed, while the damper contacts the strings and starts to dampen them.
Step 10: The key and hammer return to their at-rest positions.

20 Three Adjustments on the Key

Terminology to Remember

Table 20.1 US and UK terms (differences in bold)

USA	UK
Key height	Key height
Key dip	Key dip
Lost motion	**Waste touch**
Balance rail punchings	**Balance rail washers**
Front rail punchings	**Touch rail washers**
Hammer rest rail	Hammer rest rail

Take a moment and examine the key of an upright piano. Notice the three adjustment points (Figure 20.1). The first is under the front of the key, the second is under the middle of the key, and the third is the capstan.

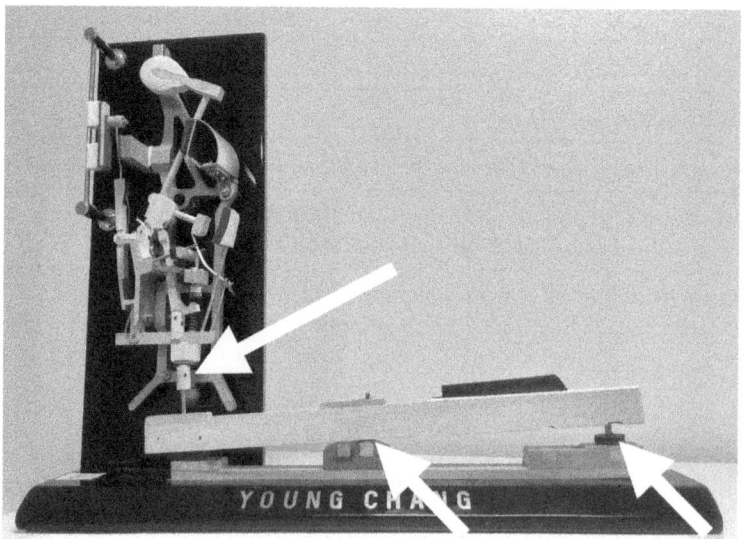

Figure 20.1 *The three adjustment points on the key.*

Key Height

Let's start with the adjustment in the middle of the key. The key pivots on a long piece of wood referred to as the balance rail. Each key is held in place by a pin on the balance rail. This pin is called the balance rail pin. Underneath the middle of each key there is a felt punching, and underneath that, there are paper or cardboard punchings. These punchings determine the height of the key when at rest. Using tweezers to remove these punchings makes it much easier.

If you want the key to be higher, then you add paper or cardboard punchings underneath the felt punching.

If you want the key to be lower, then you remove paper or cardboard punchings from underneath the felt punching.

Natural key height is measured from the bottom of the keybed (the piece of wood to which the frame for the keys is attached) to the top of the key when at rest (Figure 20.2). You will need to remove the neighboring key to get a good reading with your ruler.

Sharp key height is measured from the top of the neighboring natural keys to the top of the sharp key when at rest (Figure 20.3).

Figure 20.2 *Measuring natural key height.*

Figure 20.3 *Measuring sharp key height.*

While the range of acceptable key heights vary, the naturals tend to be somewhere around 65 millimeters. The sharps are almost always 12–13 millimeters higher than the naturals, see Table 20.2.

Key Dip (or Key Travel)

Moving on, let's look at the adjustment at the front of the key. The front of the key moves up and down on a pin inserted in a long wooden piece called the front rail. This pin is called the front rail pin. Underneath the front of each key there is a felt punching, and underneath that, there are

Table 20.2 *Natural and sharp key heights*

Regulation Point	Acceptable Range	Adjustment Location	How to Adjust
Natural key height	~65 mm	Balance rail punchings	Add punchings to increase Remove punchings to decrease
Sharp key height	12–13 mm above the naturals	Balance rail punchings	Add punchings to increase Remove punchings to decrease

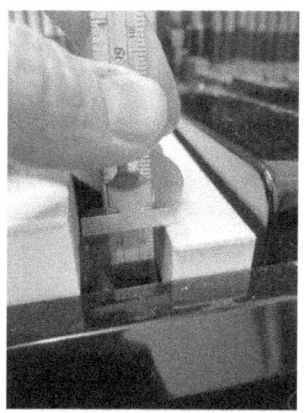

Figure 20.4 *Measuring natural key dip.*

paper or cardboard punchings. These punchings determine how far the key can be pressed down.

If less key dip is needed, add paper punchings underneath the felt punching.

If more key dip is needed, remove paper punchings from underneath the felt punching.

Key dip is measured by pressing the key down and measuring its displacement from its at-rest position (Figure 20.4). For example, if the key height is 64 millimeters and the key is pressed down and measured at 54 millimeters, then the key dip is 10 millimeters (64 millimeters minus 54 millimeters).

Natural key dip tends to be very close to 10 millimeters. Sharp key dip is usually set to meet the demands of aftertouch (which we will cover in an upcoming lesson), see Table 20.3.

Table 20.3 *Natural and sharp key dip*

Regulation Point	Acceptable Range	Adjustment Location	How to Adjust
Natural key dip	~10 mm	Front rail punchings	Add punchings to decrease Remove punchings to increase
Sharp key dip	Set to aftertouch	Front rail punchings	Add punchings to decrease Remove punchings to increase

Lost Motion

Figure 20.5 *Notice the gap between the top of the jack and the hammer butt. This indicates a fair amount of lost motion.*

The final adjustment on the key is made at the capstan. As we learned in the last lesson, the capstan is the contact point between the key and the wippen. Another contact point is the jack and the hammer butt. Looking at the big picture, we can see how adjusting the capstan controls the location of the jack in relation to the hammer butt. Notice the gap between the top of the jack and the hammer butt in Figure 20.5.

The lower the capstan, the farther the jack is from the hammer butt.

The higher the capstan, the closer the jack is to the hammer butt.

Turn the capstan counterclockwise to raise the capstan (and the jack).

Turn the capstan clockwise to lower the capstan (and the jack).

Lost motion is felt by pushing the key down very slowly. The jack should move only slightly before contacting the hammer butt. If the jack moves a large distance before engaging the hammer butt, then the key movement up until that point is wasted, or "lost."

So why not just raise the jack until it touches the hammer butt? This isn't ideal either. In an upright piano, the hammers were designed to rest on the long rail that holds them in place when not in use. This rail is called the hammer rest rail.

If the jack is too high, then the hammer butt will be resting on the jack, not the hammer rest rail. You can test for this by gently pulling the hammer rest rail toward you (Figure 20.6). The hammers should follow the rest rail. If they don't, then you know that the jacks are too high.

Video 20.1 shows how to adjust for lost motion on a single note.

Figure 20.6 *Pulling the hammer rest rail to check for any capstans that are too high. For example, the fourth hammer from the right in this photograph did not follow the rest rail like the first three hammers did.*

♪ **Video 20.1—Setting lost motion.**

One last thing before the Hands-on Homework: Upright pianos come with two common styles of capstans. This means you will need two different capstan wrenches (Figures 20.7 and 20.8).

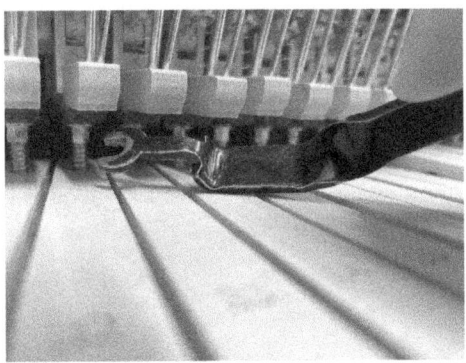

Figure 20.7 *The two types of upright capstans and their tools.*

Figure 20.8 *The two types of upright capstans and their tools.*

Table 20.4 *Lost motion*

Regulation Point	Acceptable Range	Adjustment Location	How to Adjust
Lost Motion	A small amount before the hammer is engaged	Capstan	Turn counterclockwise to raise the jack Turn clockwise to lower the jack

Hands-on Homework: *Measure the height of a key on your practice piano. Then press the key down and measure where it stops. Subtract that number from the key height to calculate the key dip.*

Then check the note for lost motion by pressing the key slowly. Does the jack move a fair amount before it engages the hammer? If so, then the capstan needs to be raised.

If it seems like the hammer moves at the same time as the jack, then pull back gently on the hammer rest rail. The hammer should follow the rest rail. If not, then introduce a small amount of lost motion in the note by lowering the capstan using the appropriate capstan regulating tool.

Repeat this process on two other notes, measuring their key height and key dip, then setting the lost motion.

21 Three Measurements from the Hammer to the Strings

Terminology to Remember

Table 21.1 US and UK terms (differences in bold)

USA	UK
Blow distance	**Blow**
Let-off	**Set off**
Checking	Checking
Hammer rest rail	Hammer rest rail
Let-off button	**Set-off button**
Jack toe, or jack tender	Jack toe, or jack tender
Backcheck	**Check**

Now that we are familiar with the three adjustment points on the key, let's examine three measurements we can take from the hammer to the string at different moments in the keystroke.

Blow Distance

The blow distance is how far the hammer is from the strings when the hammer is at rest. To measure, simply take your ruler and see how far the strings are from the closest point of the hammer (Figure 21.1). This is usually around 45 millimeters ± 2 millimeters.

On an upright piano, the blow distance is adjusted for all the hammers at once. This is done by inserting a piece of felt

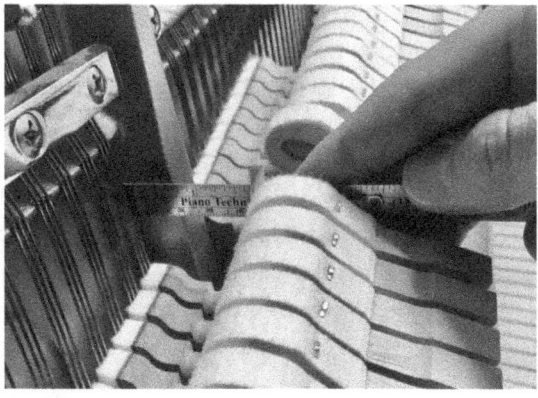

Figure 21.1 *Measuring the blow distance.*

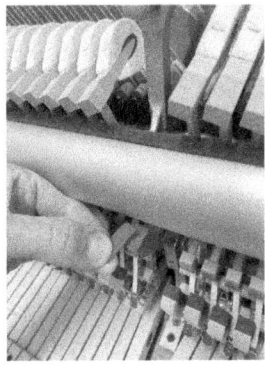

Figure 21.2 *Adjusting the blow distance. Notice the small piece of felt in my fingers.*

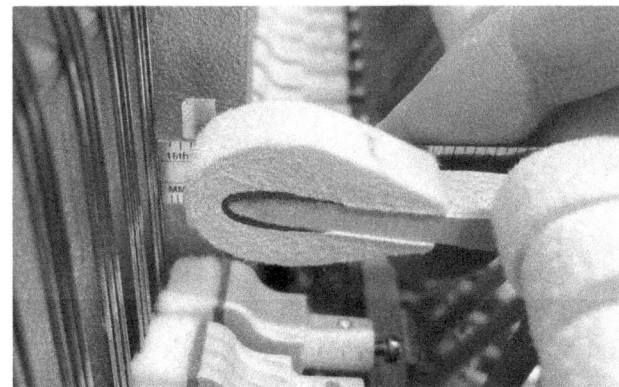

Figure 21.3 *Measuring the let-off.*

underneath the hammer rest rail to move the hammers closer to the strings, or by removing a piece of felt to move the hammers farther from the strings (Figure 21.2).

Table 21.2 *The blow distance*

Regulation Point	Acceptable Range	Adjustment Location	How to Adjust
Blow distance	45 mm ± 2	Hammer rest rail	Add felts underneath to decrease Remove felts underneath to increase

Let-off

If you play the key *very* slowly, then the hammer should move toward the strings until it almost touches them. Then, when the hammer is only a small distance away from the strings, it will change direction and fall back. Let-off is measured as that tiny distance between the hammer and the strings just before the hammer falls back.

To measure this, hold the ruler by the strings as the hammer moves slowly forward. Then observe when the hammer changes directions. The distance from the strings to the hammer at that moment is the let-off (Figure 21.3). It is usually around 2 millimeters.

Why is the hammer changing directions? It all has to do with escapement, which was mentioned back in Lesson 19. The jack is pushing the hammer toward the strings until at a certain point the toe of the jack contacts the let-off button. This causes the jack to swing out from under the hammer butt. In a normal keystroke, the hammer would then be free to strike the strings. Because we are playing the key very slowly, the hammer doesn't have enough momentum to strike the strings. Instead, we observe this moment of escapement as the jack swinging out from under the hammer, which in turn causes the hammer to change directions and fall back.

With this in mind, we can see how adjusting the moment at which the jack toe contacts the let-off button will increase or decrease how close the hammer gets to the strings before it falls back. This will require the use of a let-off regulation tool (Figure 21.4). This tool is often used in a combination handle, which allows for different tips to be attached as needed. Each tip has a different function.

To increase the let-off, turn the eyelet screw for the let-off button clockwise. This moves the let-off button closer to the jack toe, which results in the jack swinging out from under the hammer butt sooner. This means that the hammer will be farther from the strings when it changes direction.

To decrease the let-off, turn the eyelet screw for the let-off button counterclockwise. This moves the let-off button farther away from the jack toe, which results in the jack swinging out from under the hammer butt later. This means that the hammer will be closer to the strings when it changes directions.

Those last two paragraphs might have been a little hard to follow. Watch Video 21.1 and then try reading them again to solidify your understanding.

Figure 21.4 *Adjusting the let-off.*

♪ **Video 21.1—Adjusting the let-off.**

Table 21.3 *Let-off*

Regulation Point	Acceptable Range	Adjustment Location	How to Adjust
Let-off	2 mm	Let-off button	Turn counterclockwise to decrease Turn clockwise to increase

Checking

The final measurement from the hammer to the strings is called checking. To make this measurement you will need to press a key with a medium blow and hold the key down. The catcher on the hammer assembly should now be in contact with the backcheck. Piano technicians refer to this position as the hammer being "in check."

To measure the checking distance, put the hammer in check, then use your ruler to measure the distance from the strings to the closest part of the hammer (Figure 21.5). The ballpark range for this measurement is usually around 12–16 millimeters.

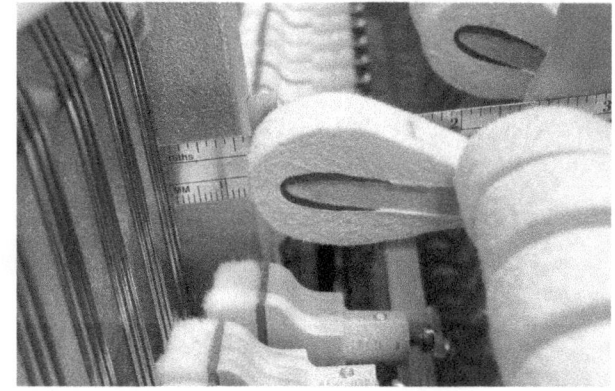

Figure 21.5 *Measuring the checking distance.*

To adjust, simply use your fingers to bend the backcheck toward the hammer, or away from the hammer. As you do so, use your other hand to hold the wippen in place (Figure 21.6).

Bend the backcheck toward the hammer to decrease the checking distance (make the hammer check closer to the strings).

Bend the backcheck away from the hammer to increase the checking distance (make the hammer check farther from the strings).

Note: The checking distance in upright pianos is notoriously inconsistent. If you play the key harder or softer, then the checking distance will change slightly. It's nice to be aware of this so you don't beat yourself up. It's not you, it's just the backcheck.

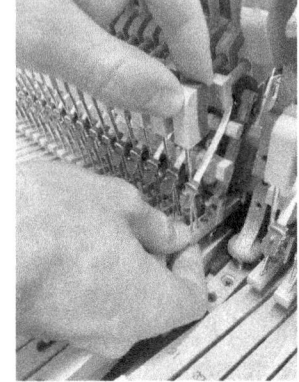

Figure 21.6 *Adjusting the checking distance. Notice how I am supporting the wippen.*

Table 21.4 *Checking*

Regulation Point	Acceptable Range	Adjustment Location	How to Adjust
Checking	12–16 mm	Backcheck	Bend toward the hammer to decrease Bend away from the hammer to increase

Figures 21.7, 21.8 and 21.9 depict all three measurements from the hammer to the string so you can visualize each one.

Hands-on Homework: *Measure the blow distance, let-off and checking for three notes on your piano. Then do your best to adjust the let-off to 2 millimeters for those notes. Finally, set the checking to 15 millimeters on those three notes.*

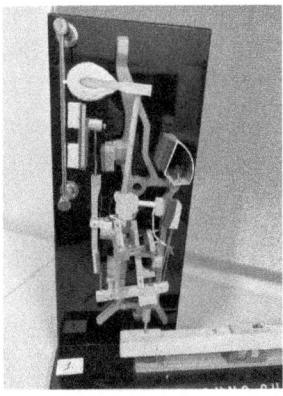

Figure 21.7 *Let-off.*

Figure 21.8 *Checking.*

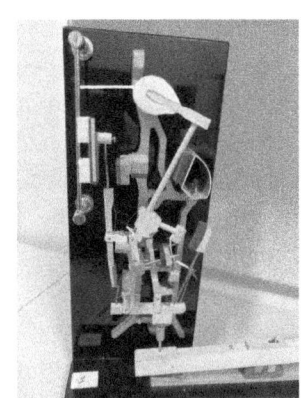

Figure 21.9 *Blow distance.*

22 Upright Aftertouch

Terminology to Remember

Table 22.1 *US and UK terms*

USA	UK
Aftertouch	Aftertouch
Aftertouch gap	Aftertouch gap

We have now learned the three adjustments on the key:

1. Key height
2. Key dip
3. Lost motion

We have also learned the three measurements from the hammer to the strings:

1. Blow distance
2. Let-off
3. Checking

Is that all there is to it? If those regulation points are adjusted to their ballpark ranges, then does that mean that the piano is regulated? Not necessarily. Certainly, if the regulation points on a piano measure outside of these ballpark ranges, then reigning them in will help immensely.

Over time, the felt and leather in the action will compress with use and age. Wood in the action will expand and contract with seasonal changes. As a result, a piano action will need to be regulated periodically to maintain its optimal level of performance.

Perhaps the most useful framework for achieving this optimal regulation is aftertouch. Aftertouch is the cumulative result of all six of the regulation points we have considered. Strictly defined, it is the amount of movement left in the action parts after escapement, resulting in the clearance of the jack from the hammer assembly.

Another way of looking at this might be to ask: How far does the key move after let-off? If the key dip is 10 millimeters, then we typically want let-off to happen around the 8.5 millimeter mark. Meaning that the last 1.5 millimeters of the key dip occurs *after* the hammer escapes and the note is played. We also want to ensure that the jack clears the hammer assembly when the hammer is caught by the backcheck.

This extra movement allows the action parts to complete their full cycle and reset for the next blow.

Too little or no aftertouch and the jack won't allow the hammer to check properly, often resulting in double-striking hammers (see Video 22.1).

♪ **Video 22.1—Double striking hammers on an upright piano.**

Before we can determine if a note has the correct amount of aftertouch, we must first get all six regulation points into their ballpark ranges. Let's work through this step by step.

1. Decide on a key height. For simplicity, let's just use what's there without any adjustment.
2. Add or remove front rail punchings to set the key dip to 10 millimeters.
3. Address the lost motion, if needed, by turning the capstan.
4. Set the let-off to 2 millimeters.
5. Set the checking to 15 millimeters.

The final regulation point is the blow distance. While we could simply set this distance to 45 millimeters, a better approach would be to use aftertouch to help us determine what blow distance the piano wants.

Figure 22.1 *Notice the small gap between the top of the jack and the hammer butt. This means the note has the correct amount of aftertouch.*

Before moving the hammer rest rail to adjust the blow distance, play a note and hold it down (put the hammer in check). Then look at the relationship between the top of the jack and the hammer butt. There should be a small gap (Figure 22.1). If there is no gap, then that means that this note doesn't have enough aftertouch (Figure 22.2). If there is a large gap, then that means that this note has too much aftertouch (Figure 22.3).

I like to refer to the gap between the top of the jack and the hammer butt as the aftertouch gap.

If you see a small aftertouch gap, then that is the piano's

way of telling you that the blow distance is in the right place.

If your piano hasn't been regulated in a while, then likely you will see no aftertouch gap, which is the piano's way of telling you that it needs more aftertouch.

To add more aftertouch you can move the hammers closer to the strings by adding felt under the hammer rest rail.

But wait, there is a chain reaction that occurs from this! If you move the hammer rest rail forward, then the jack is no longer close to the hammer butt, which means that the lost motion needs to be addressed again.

You also need to set the checking to 15mm again.

The entire process looks like this:

Figure 22.2 *No gap between the top of the jack and the hammer butt. This means the note needs more aftertouch.*

1. Move the hammer rest rail forward by inserting a felt underneath the hammer rest rail.
2. Turn the capstan counterclockwise to remove the lost motion.
3. Reset the checking to 15 millimeters.

Once you've worked through the chain reaction, you can put the hammer in check again and look for an aftertouch gap between the top of the jack and hammer butt.

If there is a gap, then you know that this blow distance is correct. If there still isn't a gap, then add another felt under the hammer rest rail and follow the chain reaction again.

You can repeat this process until an aftertouch gap is present, but keep in mind that the ballpark range for the blow distance was 45 millimeters ± 2 millimeters. If you keep moving the hammers closer to the strings, then you risk leaving that ballpark range.

Let's say your blow distance is 43 millimeters and you still have no aftertouch gap. In this case, you'll need to remove a front rail punching to increase the key dip to be slightly past 10 millimeters. Increasing the key dip is another way of increasing the amount of aftertouch.

But wait, there is a chain reaction from this too! This one is not quite as long, but it is still important:

1. Adjust the key dip.
2. Reset the checking to 15 millimeters.

Once you've increased the key dip and reset the checking to 15 millimeters, put the hammer in check and see if there is an aftertouch gap.

At a certain point, the blow distance and key dip will balance until the aftertouch gap between the jack and the hammer butt is present (when the hammer is in check). That means that those values are correct for your piano.

There is a lot going on here. Watching Video 22.2 should help clear things up. As with the lessons on tuning, this lesson will take some practice before understanding truly sets in.

♪ **Video 22.2—Setting upright aftertouch.**

Figure 22.3 *A large gap between the top of the jack and the hammer butt. This means the note has too much aftertouch.*

Table 22.2 *Upright aftertouch*

Regulation Point	Acceptable Range	Adjustment Location	How to Adjust
Upright aftertouch	A small gap between the top of the jack and the hammer butt (when the hammer is in check)	Blow distance and key dip	Decrease blow distance to increase aftertouch Increase blow distance to decrease aftertouch (Be sure to address lost motion and checking) Increase key dip to increase aftertouch Decrease key dip to decrease aftertouch (Be sure to address checking)

Hands-on Homework: *Work through the following procedure on one note of your piano.*

1. *Decide on a key height. For simplicity, just use what's there without any adjustment.*
2. *Add or remove front rail punchings to set the key dip to 10 millimeters.*
3. *Address the lost motion, if needed, by turning the capstan.*
4. *Set the let-off to 2 millimeters.*
5. *Set the checking to 15 millimeters.*

6 Put the hammer in check and look for an aftertouch gap.

7 If no gap is present, then insert a felt underneath the hammer rest rail to move the hammers closer to the strings.

   a Address the lost motion.

   b Reset the checking to 15 millimeters.

8 Put the hammer in check and look for an aftertouch gap.

9 If needed, move the hammer rest rail again or remove a front rail punching to increase the key dip until an aftertouch gap is present.

   a If the hammer rest rail is moved, then address the lost motion and reset the checking.

   b If the key dip is changed, then reset the checking.

Once you reach this point, you can remove the felt you inserted and put back some lost motion in your sample note. You will also want to reset the checking on that note.

As a bonus challenge, you can leave the felt under the hammer rest rail. If you do this, then you will need to address the lost motion and the checking on every note in your piano. While this will take significantly more time, doing so will help you retain this information and improve the touch of your upright piano.

Unit 3 Exam

I hope you enjoyed this unit. In my experience, people tend to be much more excited about action regulation than they are about tuning (at least at first). Personally, I love that piano technology encompasses so many different dimensions. I feel like tuning fires up one part of my brain while regulation and repair engage another.

Before moving to grand regulation, let's make sure we have internalized what we've learned together in this unit by reviewing the terminology and regulation points of the upright piano action. Much of what we have learned here is built upon in the next unit, so a solid foundational knowledge of these terms, tools, and techniques is critical.

Once you feel ready, take the Unit 3 Exam below. The answers can be found in the answer key at the end of this book. For the best results, I'd recommend taking this exam in front of your practice piano. Do not look up the answers in the book as you go. Instead, reason through each question by referencing the piano itself.

Terminology from Unit 3

USA	UK (differences in bold)
Aftertouch	Aftertouch
Aftertouch gap	Aftertouch gap
Backcheck	**Check**
Balance rail punchings	**Balance rail washers**
Blow distance	**Blow**
Capstan	Capstan
Catcher	**Balance hammer**
Checking	Checking
Damper	Damper
Damper spoon	Damper spoon
Front rail punchings	**Touch rail washers**

USA	UK (differences in bold)
Hammer	Hammer
Hammer butt	Hammer butt
Hammer rest rail	Hammer rest rail
Jack	Jack
Jack toe, or jack tender	Jack toe, or jack tender
Key	Key
Key dip	Key dip
Key height	Key height
Let-off	**Set off**
Let-off button	**Set-off button**
Lost motion	**Waste touch**
Wippen	**Lever**

Regulation Points from Unit 3

Regulation Point	Acceptable Range	Adjustment Location	How to Adjust
Natural key height	~65 mm	Balance rail punchings	Add punchings to increase Remove punchings to decrease
Sharp key height	12–13 mm above the naturals	Balance rail punchings	Add punchings to increase Remove punchings to decrease
Natural key dip	~10 mm	Front rail punchings	Add punchings to decrease Remove punchings to increase
Sharp key dip	Set to aftertouch	Front rail punchings	Add punchings to decrease Remove punchings to increase
Lost motion	A small amount before the hammer is engaged	Capstan	Turn counterclockwise to raise the jack Turn clockwise to lower the jack
Blow distance	45 mm ± 2 mm	Hammer rest rail	Add felts underneath to decrease Remove felts underneath to increase
Let-off	2 mm	Let-off button	Turn counterclockwise to decrease Turn clockwise to increase
Checking	12–16 mm	Backcheck	Bend toward the hammer to decrease Bend away from the hammer to increase

Regulation Point	Acceptable Range	Adjustment Location	How to Adjust
Upright aftertouch	A small gap between the top of the jack and the hammer butt (when the hammer is in check)	Blow distance and key dip	Decrease blow distance to increase aftertouch Increase blow distance to decrease aftertouch (Be sure to address lost motion and checking) Increase key dip to increase aftertouch Decrease key dip to decrease aftertouch (Be sure to address checking)

Unit 3 Exam

1 The capstan contacts …

    a the hammer butt

    b the wippen

    c the damper

2 The jack contacts …

    a the hammer butt

    b the wippen

    c the damper

3 The damper spoon contacts …

    a the hammer butt

    b the wippen

    c the damper

4 Escapement begins when these two action parts touch. Select the two that apply:

    a The jack toe

    b The wippen

    c The capstan

    d The let-off button

    e The backcheck

    f The catcher

5   When the catcher is in contact with the backcheck, technicians refer to the hammer as being …

   a   caught
   b   captured
   c   in check
   d   locked in
   e   backchecked

6   Connect the regulation point to where its adjustment is made:

Key Dip (Key Travel)	Capstan
Key height	Front rail punchings
Lost motion	Balance rail punchings
Let-off	Backcheck
Checking	Hammer rest rail
Blow distance	Let-off button

7   True or False:

   In an upright piano, the blow distance can be adjusted for an individual hammer.

8   When blow distance is adjusted, what two things need to be reset?

   a   Lost motion and checking
   b   Lost motion and key dip
   c   Let-off and key dip
   d   Let-off and checking

9   When key dip is adjusted, what needs to be reset?

   a   Let-off
   b   Lost motion
   c   Key height
   d   Checking

10 True or False:

   If the hammers in an upright piano are double-striking, then the piano does not have enough aftertouch.

UNIT 4

Grand Regulation

Tools You Will Need

Tools to Buy:

- Balance rail punchings*
- Front rail punchings*
- 8-inch tweezers*
- Millimeter ruler with slide*
- Capstan regulator*

- Grand let-off regulating screwdriver
- Drop screwdriver
- Regulating screwdriver
- Spring tool

*Indicates tools also used for upright regulation.

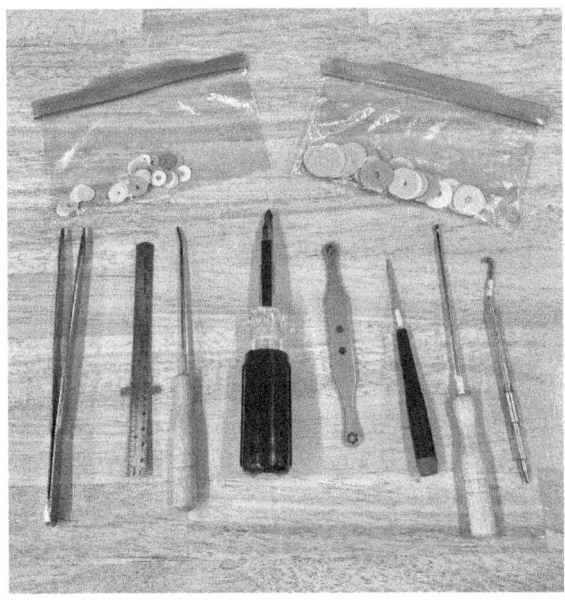

A Few Notes on this Unit

As exciting as it was to learn about how to regulate an upright piano, sadly, it is pretty rare for a technician to take on a full upright regulation job. The most frequent upright regulation complaint is that the hammers are double-striking. This is so common that we will revisit the subject as a repair in Lesson 32.

Grand pianos, on the other hand, are regulated *much* more often. In part because grand piano owners tend to be more serious players. It is therefore well worth immersing yourself in the lessons that follow. Being able to offer services beyond just tuning will make you a more marketable technician and will make working on pianos far more enjoyable.

Just bear in mind that this unit does not seek to guide you through an entire regulation procedure. Instead, it focuses on familiarizing you with the points of regulation on a single note.

23 The Grand Keystroke

Terminology to Remember

Table 23.1 US and UK terms (differences in bold)

USA	UK
Key	Key
Wippen	**Lever**
Damper	Damper
Hammer	Hammer
Capstan	Capstan
Jack	Jack
Hammer knuckle	**Roller**
Let-off button	**Set-off button**
Backcheck	**Check**

The grand piano action has the same four main components as the upright piano. These are:

1 The key (which is pressed by the player).
2 The hammer (which strikes the strings).
3 The damper (which dampens the strings).
4 The wippen (which connects the key movement to the hammer).

There are also three main contact points between the action parts (Figure 23.1). These points differ slightly from those of an upright piano.

1 The capstan (on the key) contacts the wippen.
2 The jack (on the wippen) contacts the hammer knuckle.
3 The back of the key contacts the damper underlever.

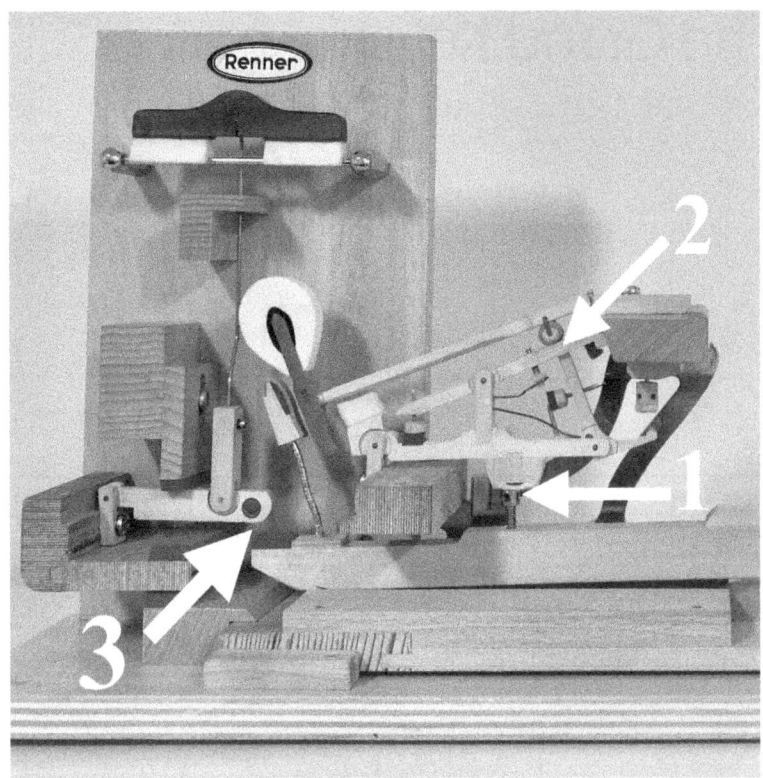

Figure 23.1 Grand action contact points.

Let's take a closer look at each of these components and how they interact.

The key is a simple lever. When you press the front of the key down, the back of the key moves up. There is a capstan on the back of the key that communicates the key movement to the wippen. This contact point is labeled 1 in Figure 23.1.

As the capstan moves the wippen, the jack contacts the hammer knuckle and starts to move the hammer toward the strings. This contact point is labeled 2 in Figure 23.1.

When the hammer is about halfway to the strings, the back of the key engages the damper underlever, which causes the damper to be lifted off the strings. This contact point is labeled 3 in Figure 23.1. This contact point is different from the upright piano, which uses a spoon attached to the wippen to engage the damper.

Just before the hammer strikes the strings, the toe of the jack contacts the let-off button (Figure 23.2). This causes the jack to swing out from under the hammer knuckle. This moment is called escapement. The hammer is now propelled the last few millimeters toward the strings (see Video 23.1).

♪ **Video 23.1—Escapement in a grand piano.**

Figure 23.2 *How escapement works on a grand piano. The bottom arrow points at the jack toe. The top arrow points at the let-off button. When those two pieces touch, it starts to move the jack out from underneath the hammer assembly.*

Figure 23.3 *The hammer is "in check." Meaning that the note has been played, the key is held down, and the tail of the hammer is in contact with the backcheck.*

After the hammer hits the strings, it rebounds and is caught by the backcheck (which is attached to the back of the key). As long as the key is held down, the tail of the hammer will remain in contact with the backcheck. Technicians refer to this position as the hammer being "in check." See Figure 23.3.

When the key is released, the jack returns under the hammer knuckle so that the key can be played again. The damper then contacts the strings to dampen the note. Finally, the hammer and key return to their rest positions.

Hands-on Homework: *Pull the action of your practice grand piano (review Lesson 6, if needed). Play a note slowly and observe the action parts in motion. Make note of each step in Table 23.2 as you see it take effect. Note that you will not be able to see the dampers lift with the action outside of the piano.*

After making your observations, take out a piece of paper and try to list the grand keystroke steps from memory. Don't move on until you can get them all in the correct order.

Table 23.2 *The grand keystroke step by step*

Step 1: The player presses a key.
Step 2: The capstan starts to lift the wippen causing the jack to contact the hammer knuckle, moving the hammer toward the string.
Step 3: When the hammer is about halfway to the string, the back of the key starts to lift the damper off the strings.
Step 4: The jack toe contacts the let-off button causing the jack to no longer contact the hammer knuckle.
Step 5: The hammer strikes the strings!
Step 6: The hammer rebounds and is caught by the backcheck (on the back of the key).
Step 7: The key is released by the player.
Step 8: The jack quickly returns to its position under the hammer knuckle ready to play the next note, if needed.
Step 9: The damper contacts the strings and starts to dampen them.
Step 10: The key and hammer return to their at-rest positions.

24 Three Adjustments on the Wippen

Terminology to Remember

Table 24.1 *US and UK terms (differences in bold)*

USA	UK
Jack position	Jack position
Repetition lever height	Repetition lever height
Spring tension	Spring tension
Jack	Jack
Hammer knuckle	**Roller**
Repetition lever	Repetition lever

Hopefully reading through the last lesson showed you that the upright and grand piano keystrokes are fairly similar. While their respective actions feature some minor differences, both uprights and grands share the same main components. In this lesson we will focus on the unique features of the grand wippen.

Figure 24.1 compares a wippen from an upright piano to a wippen from a grand piano. Notice that other than the jack and the piece on the bottom that rests on the capstan, the two wippens look quite different. The upright wippen (on the top in Figure 24.1) contains a backcheck and a damper spoon. On a grand piano, the dampers are lifted by the back of the keys, and the backchecks are attached to the backs of the keys as well. This frees up the grand wippen to include new adjustment points that are unique to the grand piano. Let's examine each one.

Figure 24.1 *An upright wippen (above) and a grand wippen (below).*

Jack Position

In a grand piano the position of the jack can be adjusted to ensure that it engages the hammer at the optimal position. The

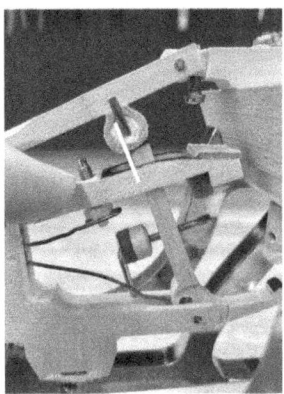

Figure 24.2 *The back of the jack should align with the back of the knuckle core. Notice the white line.*

jack should be perpendicular to the hammer shank (the piece of wood to which the hammer is attached). On most grand pianos, the easiest way to accomplish this is to align the back of the jack (the side away from the player) with the back of the wood knuckle core as shown in Figure 24.2.

To adjust the position of the jack, use a regulating screwdriver to turn the jack regulating screw (Figure 24.3).

Turn the screw clockwise to move the jack toward the player.

Turn the screw counterclockwise to move the jack away from the player.

To observe if the jack is in the correct place, lift up the neighboring hammers and press down the repetition lever for the note you are regulating with your finger. The repetition lever is the piece of wood through which the jack travels.

Then look at the jack from the side. To ensure that you are looking at the jack from the correct angle, move your eyes until you can see the black marking on the back of the jack (the side away from the player). Then move your eyes until that black marking is no longer visible. Examine the jack from this angle to see if the back of the jack is aligned with the back of the knuckle core. See Figures 24.4 and 24.5, as well as Video 24.1.

Figure 24.3 *The jack regulating screw. Notice how I need to slide my tool in from the front, in between the let-off buttons to access the screw.*

Figure 24.4 *Notice the black marking on the back of the jack.*

Figure 24.5 *The black marking is no longer visible.*

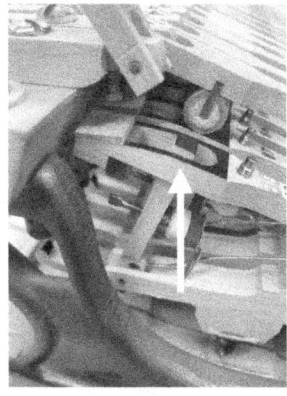

Figure 24.6 *The repetition lever is too low. The jack appears to be "sticking out."*

🎵 **Video 24.1—Move your vantage point to ensure that you are looking at the jack from the correct angle.**

Table 24.2 *Jack position*

Regulation Point	Acceptable Range	Adjustment Location	How to Adjust
Jack position	The back of the jack should be aligned with the back of the knuckle core	The jack regulating screw	Turn the screw clockwise to move the jack closer to the player Turn the screw counterclockwise to move the jack away from the player

Repetition Lever Height

The repetition lever is one of the key reasons a grand piano action outperforms an upright piano action. This lever plays a critical role in improving the speed of repetition and level of control the pianist feels.

The height of the repetition lever relative to the jack can be adjusted. If it is too low, the jack will be sticking out (Figure 24.6). This makes it harder for the jack to return under the hammer knuckle, which negatively impacts repetition.

If the repetition lever is too high, then the jack is buried (Figure 24.7) and small amounts of lost motion are introduced to the system, which negatively impacts control.

The goal is therefore to have the repetition lever just high enough to allow the jack to return freely, but no more.

Figure 24.7 *The repetition lever is too high. The jack is buried.*

To adjust the height of the repetition lever, use a regulating screwdriver to turn the repetition lever regulating screw (Figure 24.8).

Turn the screw clockwise to lower the repetition lever.

Turn the screw counterclockwise to raise the repetition lever.

When turning the screw, be sure to lift up the back of the repetition lever slightly so that the felt of the regulating button doesn't rub against the felt on the back of the wippen (Figure 24.9).

To make sure the repetition lever height is set correctly, press down on the jack toe with your finger, then release the jack. Does the jack return on its own? The jack should spring back under the hammer knuckle. Let me explain how this process works.

Figure 24.8 *The repetition lever regulating screw.*

Start by turning the repetition lever regulating screw clockwise until the jack no longer returns when it is manually pressed down and then released.

Then turn the regulating screw counterclockwise in small amounts until the jack returns fully when it is manually pressed down and then released.

If you aren't sure if the jack has returned fully, then you can tap on the repetition lever with your tool and watch the jack for any movement.

Watch Video 24.2 for a demonstration of this process.

🎵 **Video 24.2—Setting the repetition lever height.**

Figure 24.9 *Lifting up on the regulating button when adjusting.*

If everything is set correctly, then the repetition lever will end up just slightly above the top of the jack. This assumes that the repetition lever is pinned to the correct amount of friction and that the spring tension is correct. Again, a regulation procedure will come with additional training. Our goal is simply to learn that these regulations points exist. Repinning an action center is beyond the scope of this book.

Table 24.3 *Repetition lever height*

Regulation Point	Acceptable Range	Adjustment Location	How to Adjust
Repetition lever height	The repetition lever should be just high enough to allow the jack to return freely	The repetition lever regulating screw	Turn the screw clockwise to lower the repetition lever Turn the screw counterclockwise to raise the repetition lever

Spring Tension

The final adjustment on the wippen is spring tension. Notice the spring in the wippen. The top section of the spring supports the repetition lever, the bottom section of the spring is connected to the jack (Figure 24.10).

This spring plays a critical role in optimizing the efficiency of the grand piano action. To understand this, we can put the hammer "in check" by pressing the key and holding it down so that the hammer tail remains in contact with the backcheck. Notice what happens to the repetition lever. It is now slightly depressed, causing the spring to be compressed. Imagine a chip clip. When you press it down, its spring also compresses. When you release the clip, it quickly springs closed. The same is true for the spring in the wippen, except that the weight of the hammer causes much of the force of the spring to be sent downward. This means that as the spring expands, it pushes the back of the key down, while at the same time, holding the hammer in place momentarily and pulling the jack back underneath the hammer knuckle. All of this happens within the blink of an eye when you release a key. Video 24.3 shows this happening in slow motion. This video was produced by Scott Murphy, RPT at the Juilliard School.

♪ **Video 24.3—Releasing a key in slow motion.**

Figure 24.10 *The spring in the grand wippen.*

If the spring is weak, then it won't perform its intended function optimally, resulting in problems with repetition. If the spring is too strong, then the hammer will resist being put in check and will jump off the backcheck, resulting in problems with control.

Piano technicians have developed a test to determine if the spring tension is correct. This is done by putting the hammer in check, then letting up on the key slightly. Since we are holding the key in place, the force of the spring is instead put into the hammer, causing the hammer to rise.

Thus, the spring tension test looks like this:

1   Put the hammer in check.

2   Let up on the front of the key slightly.

3   Watch the speed at which the hammer rises.

The hammer should rise quickly, but not so fast that it bobbles at the top.
If it does bobble at the top, then the spring is too strong.
If it doesn't rise completely, then the spring is too weak.

Video 24.4 compares the spring tension of three notes, the hammer on the left doesn't rise enough. The hammer on the right bobbles at the top. The hammer in the center is, as Goldilocks would say, "just right."

♪ **Video 24.4—The speed at which the hammer rises tells us if the spring tension needs to be adjusted.**

Figure 24.11 *Strengthening the spring.*

Figure 24.12 *Weakening the spring.*

To strengthen the spring, use your spring tool to remove the spring from the wippen and bend it upward (Figure 24.11). Reinsert the spring into its slot in the wippen when you are done.

To weaken the spring, use your spring tool to remove the spring from the wippen and push it downward (Figure 24.12). Reinsert the spring into its slot in the wippen when you are done.

This adjustment can be tricky. You will learn with experience how much bending is needed to achieve optimal results. Video 24.5 shows these spring adjustment techniques.

♪ **Video 24.5—Adjusting spring tension.**

Table 24.4 *Spring tension*

Regulation Point	Acceptable Range	Adjustment Location	How to Adjust
Spring tension	From check, when the key is lifted slightly, the hammer should rise completely without a bobble at the top	The repetition spring	Bend the spring up to strengthen Bend the spring down to weaken

Hands-on Homework: *Start by setting spring tension on a sample note in your piano so that the hammer rises quickly without a bobble at the top. For this to work, the hammer needs to be able to be "in check." You may need to adjust the backcheck forward or backward with your finger until the hammer checks.*

Next, set the jack position to align the back side of the jack (the side away from the player) with the back side of the hammer knuckle core.

Finally, set the repetition lever height so that it is just high enough for the jack to return freely.

Repeat this process on at least two other notes in your piano until the three adjustments on the wippen start to feel more approachable to you.

25 Four Measurements from the Hammer to the Strings

Terminology to Remember

Table 25.1 *US and UK terms (differences in bold)*

USA	UK
Blow distance	**Blow**
Let-off	**Set off**
Drop	Drop
Checking	Checking
Capstan	Capstan
Let-off button	**Set-off Button**
Drop screw	Drop screw
Backcheck	**Check**

In Lesson 22 we learned about the three measurements from the hammer to the strings in an upright piano, which were:

1. Blow distance
2. Let-off
3. Checking

In the grand piano, these three measurements are still used, but there is an additional fourth measurement to consider:

4. Drop

Let's examine each of these measurements.

Blow Distance

The blow distance is how far the hammer is from the strings when the hammer is at rest. You can measure this distance with a ruler, just know that it is difficult to do this with a great deal of accuracy through the strings. This distance is usually around 46 millimeters ± 2 millimeters.

That is where the similarities end between the blow distance of an upright and a grand piano.

For one, the blow distance in a grand piano can be adjusted on each individual hammer. In an upright piano, all the hammers are moved together by adjusting the hammer rest rail.

In an upright piano, the hammers should be in contact with the hammer rest rail. In a grand piano, however, the hammers should be slightly above the rest rail, or rest cushions (see Figure 25.1).

The adjustment point for the blow distance in a grand piano is the capstan (Figure 25.2).

Turn the capstan clockwise to lower the hammer (increase the blow distance).

Turn the capstan counterclockwise to raise the hammer (decrease the blow distance).

Figure 25.1 *Hammers in a grand piano should not rest on the rest cushions. Notice the space indicated by the arrow.*

Figure 25.2 *Adjusting the blow distance on a grand piano.*

Table 25.2 *Blow distance*

Regulation Point	Acceptable Range	Adjustment Location	How to Adjust
Blow distance	46 mm ± 2 mm	Capstan	Turn clockwise to increase Turn counterclockwise to decrease

Let-off

Let-off on a grand piano is nearly identical to an upright piano.

If you play the key *very* slowly, then the hammer should move toward the strings until it almost touches them. When the hammer is only a small distance away from the strings, it should then fall down slightly. Let-off is measured as that tiny distance between the hammer and the strings just before the hammer falls back down. It is usually around 2 millimeters.

Why does the hammer fall back down slightly? It all has to do with escapement, which was mentioned back in Lesson 23. The jack is pushing the hammer toward the strings, until at a certain point, the toe of the jack contacts the let-off button. This causes the jack to swing out from under the hammer knuckle. In a normal keystroke, the hammer would then be free to strike the strings. Because we are playing the key very slowly, the hammer doesn't have enough momentum to strike the strings. Instead, we observe this moment of escapement as the jack swinging out from under the hammer, which in turn causes the hammer to fall back down slightly.

We can now see how adjusting the moment at which the jack toe contacts the let-off button will either increase or decrease the proximity of the hammer to the strings before it falls back down.

While the let-off buttons on many pianos can be adjusted using a capstan tool (Figure 25.3), some pianos require a let-off regulation tool (Figure 25.4).

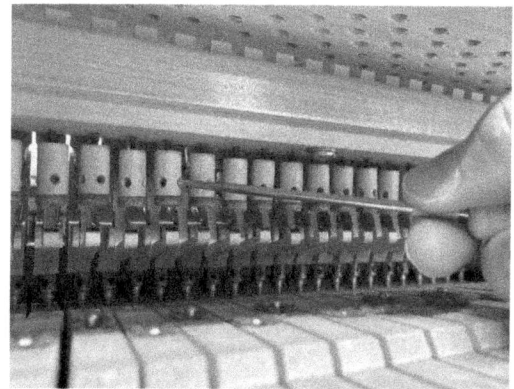

Figure 25.3 *Adjusting the let-off with a capstan tool.*

Figure 25.4 *Adjusting the let-off with a let-off regulation tool.*

To increase the let-off, turn the let-off button clockwise. This moves the let-off button closer to the jack toe, which results in the jack swinging out from under the hammer knuckle sooner. This means that the hammer will be farther away from the strings before it falls back down.

To decrease the let-off, turn the let-off button counterclockwise. This moves the let-off button farther away from the jack toe, which results in the jack swinging out from under the hammer knuckle later. This means that the hammer will be closer to the strings before it falls back down.

Note: If you can't see the hammer fall back down, then make sure you have some drop first.

Table 25.3 *Let-off*

Regulation Point	Acceptable Range	Adjustment Location	How to Adjust
Let-off	2 mm	Let-off button	Turn counterclockwise to decrease Turn clockwise to increase

Drop

Drop is unique to the grand piano. It is measured as the distance from the hammer to the strings at the moment the hammer goes through let-off and falls back down slightly.

This moment can be hard to capture because the movement of the hammer during a slow keystroke doesn't end at drop. It reaches the point of let-off, falls back down slightly, then rises slightly again.

To measure the drop, you will need to play the key slowly, watch for the moment the hammer escapes and falls back down slightly, then stop moving the key. Hold that position while you measure the drop. It is usually twice the distance of the let-off. If the let-off was 2 millimeters from the strings, then the drop should be around 4 millimeters from the strings.

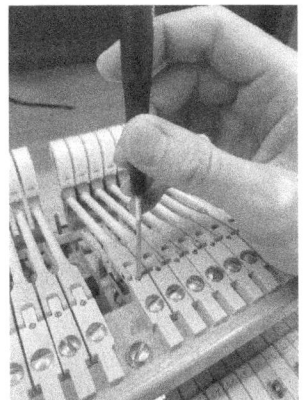

Figure 25.5 *Adjusting the drop.*

The adjustment point for the drop is called the drop screw. This screw is attached to the hammer assembly (Figure 25.5). You will need to pull the action to access the drop screws.

Turn the screw clockwise to increase the drop.

Turn the screw counterclockwise to decrease the drop.

Table 25.4 *Drop*

Regulation Point	Acceptable Range	Adjustment Location	How to Adjust
Drop	3–4 mm	Drop screw	Turn clockwise to increase Turn counterclockwise to decrease

Checking

Checking on a grand piano is very similar to an upright piano.

Press a key with a medium blow and hold the key down. The hammer tail should now be in contact with the backcheck. Piano technicians refer to this position as the hammer being "in check." Checking is measured as the distance from the hammer in check to the bottom of the strings. The ballpark range for this measurement is usually around 12–16 millimeters.

To adjust, you will first need to pull the action out onto your lap. You can now use your fingers to bend the backcheck toward the player, or away from the player (Figure 25.6).

Bend the backcheck toward the player to decrease the checking distance (make the hammer check closer to the strings).

Figure 25.6 *Adjusting the checking distance.*

Bend the backcheck away from the player to increase the checking distance (make the hammer check farther from the strings).

Table 45.5 *Checking*

Regulation Point	Acceptable Range	Adjustment Location	How to Adjust
Checking	12–16 mm	Backcheck	Bend toward the player to decrease Bend away from the player to increase

Figures 25.7, 25.8, 25.9 and 25.10 depict all four measurements from the hammer to the string so you can visualize each one.

Hands-on Homework: *Measure the blow distance, let-off, drop, and checking of three notes in your piano. Do your best to adjust the let-off to 2 millimeters for those notes. Then set the drop to 4 millimeters, and the checking to 15 millimeters for those same notes.*

Figure 25.7 *Blow distance.*

Figure 25.8 *Let-off.*

Figure 25.9 *Drop.*

Figure 25.10 *Checking.*

26 Grand Aftertouch

Terminology to Remember

Table 26.1 US and UK terms (differences in bold)

USA	UK
Key height	Key height
Key dip	Key dip
Balance rail punchings	**Balance rail washers**
Front rail punchings	**Touch rail washers**
Aftertouch	Aftertouch
Aftertouch rise	Aftertouch rise
Aftertouch gap	Aftertouch gap

We have learned the three adjustments on the wippen:

1 Jack position
2 Repetition lever height
3 Spring tension

We have also learned the four measurements from the hammer to the strings:

1 Blow distance
2 Let-off
3 Drop
4 Checking

There are two other adjustments we have yet to consider:

1 Key height
2 Key dip

Key Height

Figure 26.1 *Measuring natural key height.*

Natural key height is measured from the bottom of the keybed to the top of the key when at rest (Figure 26.1). You will need to remove the keyslip to get a good reading with your ruler.

Sharp key height is measured from the top of the neighboring natural keys to the top of the sharp key when at rest.

While the range of acceptable key heights varies, the naturals tend to be somewhere around 60 millimeters. The sharps are almost always 12–13 millimeters higher than the naturals.

Key height on a grand piano isn't as easy to adjust. You will need to remove the action stack and remove the key to access the balance rail punchings. Return the action stack to accurately see the results of this adjustment.

Table 26.2 *Natural and sharp key height*

Regulation Point	Acceptable Range	Adjustment Location	How to Adjust
Natural key height	~60 mm	Balance rail punchings	Add punchings to increase Remove punchings to decrease
Sharp key height	12–13 mm above the naturals	Balance rail punchings	Add punchings to increase Remove punchings to decrease

Key Dip (or Key Travel)

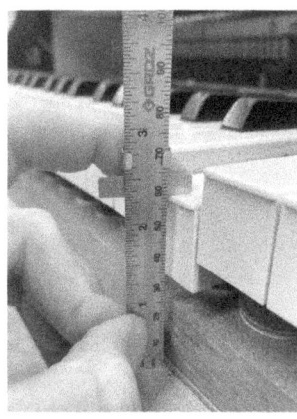

Figure 26.2 *Measuring natural key dip.*

Key dip is measured by pressing the key down and measuring its displacement from its at-rest position (Figure 26.2). For example, if the key height is 65 millimeters and the key is pressed down and measured at 55 millimeters, then the key dip is 10 millimeters (65 millimeters minus 55 millimeters).

Front rail punchings determine how far a key can be pressed down. You will need to remove the keyslip and the key stop rail to access the front rail punchings. Removing the punchings with tweezers can be helpful, especially for the sharps.

If less key dip is needed, then add paper punchings underneath the felt punching.

If more key dip if needed, then remove paper punchings from underneath the felt punching.

Natural key dip tends to be very close to 10 millimeters. Sharp key dip is usually set to meet the demands of aftertouch, which is explained below.

Table 26.3 *Natural and sharp key dip*

Regulation Point	Acceptable Range	Adjustment Location	How to Adjust
Natural key dip	~10 mm	Front rail punchings	Add punchings to decrease Remove punchings to increase
Sharp key dip	Set to aftertouch	Front rail punchings	Add punchings to decrease Remove punchings to increase

Aftertouch

Aftertouch is the amount of movement left in the action parts after escapement, resulting in the clearance of the jack from the hammer assembly.

Another way of looking at this might be to ask: How far does the key move after let-off? If the key dip is 10 millimeters, then we typically want let-off to happen around the 8.5 millimeters mark, meaning that the last 1.5 millimeters of the key dip occurs *after* the hammer escapes and the note is played. This extra movement allows the action parts to complete their full cycle and reset for the next blow.

There are three adjustment points for aftertouch. These are let-off, blow distance, and key dip. Let-off is rarely sacrificed, so that leaves us with just two options remaining.

For more aftertouch:

1 Increase the key dip
2 Decrease the blow distance (move the hammers closer to the strings)

For less aftertouch:

1 Decrease the key dip
2 Increase the blow distance (move the hammers farther away from the strings)

One of the easiest ways to know if your sample note has aftertouch is by watching the movement of the hammer after drop. During a slow key stroke, the hammer will rise, reach the point of let-off, then drop slightly. What happens next is critical.

Does the hammer rise again after drop? If so, then the note has aftertouch. If not, then the note has no aftertouch. If the hammer drops and then rises past the point of let-off, then you have too much aftertouch. Some technicians refer to this rise after drop as the "second hammer rise." I prefer the term "aftertouch rise."

What does aftertouch rise mean? It means that the hammer is still moving after escapement. The key also continues to move after escapement, as does the jack. The jack continues to move until a small aftertouch gap is present in between the top of the jack and the hammer knuckle

(Figure 26.3). This clearance was our primary focus when setting aftertouch on the upright piano. It still applies in a grand piano, but with the action in the piano, it is impossible to see. We therefore look to the aftertouch rise of the hammer to verify that an aftertouch gap is present between the jack and the knuckle. See Video 26.1.

🎵 **Video 26.1—Aftertouch rise.**

Let's see how we could adjust the blow distance to meet the demands of aftertouch:

Figure 26.3 *If the hammer has aftertouch rise, then that means that there is a gap between the jack and the hammer knuckle.*

1. Set the let-off to 2 millimeters.
2. Set the key dip to 10 millimeters.
3. Play the note slowly and look for aftertouch rise.
   a. If there is a small amount of aftertouch rise, then you are done. The blow distance is correct for this note.
   b. If there is no aftertouch rise (common on older pianos), then turn the capstan counterclockwise to raise the hammer and decrease the blow distance. This will introduce some aftertouch.
   c. If there is too much aftertouch rise (this is uncommon), then turn the capstan clockwise to lower the hammer and increase the blow distance. This will reduce the amount of aftertouch.

Video 26.2 illustrates this process.

🎵 **Video 26.2—Setting aftertouch.**

A good rule of thumb is that the hammers should be around a shank's thickness above the hammer rest rail, or rest cushions. The shank is the piece of wood to which the hammer head is attached (Figure 26.4). If there is no space between the hammer shank and the rest rail, then the piano almost certainly needs more aftertouch.

If you don't want to change the blow distance, you can also get aftertouch rise by adjusting the key dip.

Removing punchings will increase the key dip. More key dip results in more aftertouch rise.

Adding punchings will decrease the key dip. Less key dip results in less aftertouch rise.

Figure 26.4 *The hammers should not be on the rest rail, or rest cushions. If they are, then that is usually an indicator that the piano needs more aftertouch.*

Table 26.4 *Grand aftertouch*

Regulation Point	Acceptable Range	Adjustment Location	How to Adjust
Grand aftertouch	A small amount of aftertouch rise in the hammer after drop	Blow distance and key dip	Decrease blow distance to increase aftertouch Increase blow distance to decrease aftertouch Increase key dip to increase aftertouch Decrease key dip to decrease aftertouch

Hands-on Homework: *Work through the following procedure on three notes of your piano:*

1 Set the let-off to 2 millimeters.
2 Set the key dip to 10 millimeters.
3 Play the note slowly and look for aftertouch rise.
   a If there is a small amount of aftertouch rise, then you are done. The blow distance is correct for this note.
   b If there is no aftertouch rise (common on older pianos), then turn the capstan counterclockwise to raise the hammer and decrease the blow distance. This will introduce some aftertouch.
   c If there is too much aftertouch rise (uncommon), then turn the capstan clockwise to lower the hammer and increase the blow distance. This will reduce the amount of aftertouch.

Unit 4 Exam

I want to take a moment and congratulate you on making it this far. You have completed a significant milestone. You can tune an entire piano, and you are familiar with regulation adjustment locations on both an upright and a grand piano.

All the same, adjusting a handful of notes is not the same as regulating an entire piano. You will need to regulate dozens of actions before everything starts to come into focus. Completion is not mastery, and mastery will only come with experience and good mentoring.

Look for opportunities to solidify this knowledge while it is fresh in your mind. Maybe even reread Units 3 and 4 and work through each of the Hands-on Homework assignments again on your own, or better yet, with a mentor.

Once you feel ready, take the Unit 4 Exam. For the best results, I'd recommend taking this exam in front of your practice piano. Do not look up the answers in the book as you go. Instead, reason through each question by referencing the piano itself. The answers can be found in the answer key at the end of this book.

Terminology from Unit 4

USA	UK (differences in bold)
Aftertouch	Aftertouch
Aftertouch gap	Aftertouch gap
Aftertouch rise	Aftertouch rise
Backcheck	**Check**
Balance rail punchings	**Balance rail washers**
Blow distance	**Blow**
Capstan	Capstan
Checking	Checking
Damper	Damper
Drop	Drop
Drop screw	Drop screw

USA	UK (differences in bold)
Front rail punchings	**Touch rail washers**
Hammer	Hammer
Hammer knuckle	**Roller**
Jack	Jack
Jack position	Jack position
Jack toe, or jack tender	Jack toe, or jack tender
Key	Key
Key dip	Key dip
Key height	Key height
Let-off	**Set off**
Let-off button	**Set-off button**
Repetition lever	Repetition lever
Repetition lever height	Repetition lever height
Spring tension	Spring tension
Wippen	**Lever**

Regulation Points from Unit 4

Regulation Point	Acceptable Range	Adjustment Location	How to Adjust
Natural key height	~60 mm	Balance rail punchings	Add punchings to increase Remove punchings to decrease
Sharp key height	12–13 mm above the naturals	Balance rail punchings	Add punchings to increase Remove punchings to decrease
Natural key dip	~10 mm	Front rail punchings	Add punchings to decrease Remove punchings to increase
Sharp key dip	Set to aftertouch	Front rail punchings	Add punchings to decrease Remove punchings to increase
Jack position	The back of the jack should be aligned with the back of the knuckle core	The jack regulating screw	Turn the screw clockwise to move the jack closer to the player Turn the screw counterclockwise to move the jack away from the player

Regulation Point	Acceptable Range	Adjustment Location	How to Adjust
Repetition lever height	The repetition lever should be just high enough to allow the jack to return freely	The repetition lever regulating screw	Turn the screw clockwise to lower the repetition lever Turn the screw counterclockwise to raise the repetition lever
Spring tension	From check, when the key is lifted slightly, the hammer should rise completely without a bobble at the top	The repetition spring	Bend the spring up to strengthen Bend the spring down to weaken
Blow distance	46 mm ± 2 mm	Capstan	Turn clockwise to increase Turn counterclockwise to decrease
Let-off	2 mm	Let-off button	Turn counterclockwise to decrease Turn clockwise to increase
Drop	3–4 mm	Drop screw	Turn clockwise to increase Turn counterclockwise to decrease
Checking	12–16 mm	Backcheck	Bend toward the player to decrease Bend away from the player to increase
Grand aftertouch	A small amount of aftertouch rise in the hammer after drop	Blow distance and key dip	Decrease blow distance to increase aftertouch Increase blow distance to decrease aftertouch Increase key dip to increase aftertouch Decrease key dip to decrease aftertouch

Unit 4 Exam

1 The capstan contacts ...

   a The damper

   b The hammer knuckle

   c The wippen

2 The jack contacts ...

   a The damper

   b The hammer knuckle

   c The wippen

3 The back of the key contacts ...

   a The damper

   b The hammer knuckle

   c The wippen

4 Put the following moments of a slow keystroke in order:
- The hammer rises from its at-rest position
- Aftertouch rise
- Drop
- Let-off

5 When the hammer tail is in contact with the backcheck, we refer to the hammer as being …
   a Caught
   b In check
   c Captured
   d Locked in
   e Backchecked

6 The three adjustments on the grand wippen are _____, _____, and _____?

7 The four measurements from the hammer to the string in a grand piano are _____, _____, _____, and _____.

8 Connect the regulation point to where its adjustment is made:

Key Dip (Key Travel)	Repetition spring
Key height	Front rail punchings
Jack position	Balance rail punchings
Let-off	Backcheck
Drop	Capstan
Blow distance	Let-off button
Repetition lever height	Jack regulating screw
Spring tension	Repetition lever height screw
Checking	Drop screw

9 True or False:

In a grand piano, the hammers should rest on the hammer rest rail (or rest cushions).

10 Which of the following will increase aftertouch, select all that apply:
   a Increase the key dip
   b Decrease the key dip
   c Increase the blow distance (move the hammers farther away from the strings)
   d Decrease the blow distance (move the hammers closer to the strings)

UNIT 5

Voicing

Tools You Will Need

Tools to Buy:

- Chopstick needle tool
- Upright voicing tool

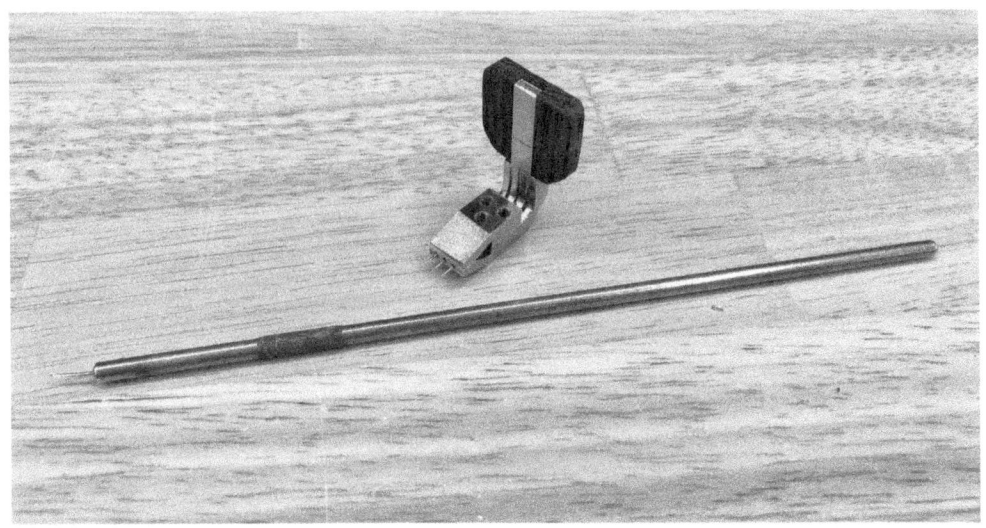

A Few Notes on this Unit

In Question 13 of *The Piano Owner's Guide* I mentioned the Three Ts of Maintenance. They are:

1 Tune

2 Touch

3 Tone

Unit 2 covered tuning. Units 3 and 4 covered regulation, which affects the touch of the piano. This unit will consider tone, which is adjusted by a process known as voicing. A comprehensive discussion of voicing is well beyond the scope of this book. Nevertheless, it would be beneficial to discuss the most common voicing procedure before moving onto repairs.

As this unit contains only one lesson, there will be no Unit Exam, only a Hands-on Homework assignment.

27 Voicing for Evenness

For a piano to perform at its best, the touch (regulation) should be consistent from note to note. The same is true for the piano's tone. If you play a chromatic scale up and down the keyboard striking each key with the same amount of force, no single note should stick out or sound accented. On most pianos, this isn't the case. Often the piano will sound more like what is depicted in Figure 27.1. The lines represent the volume of each note when played with the same amount of force.

What can be done? That's where voicing for evenness comes in.

Imagine you are driving down a mountain road and see a road slide up ahead. Before you can proceed you must first clear the boulders, then the rocks.

Do you see the boulders in Figure 27.1? I see A♯, D♯, and G♯.

Only once those notes are addressed can you properly hear the rocks. You might even find a few potholes to fill before the road looks smooth and even.

Now that you've identified the notes that stick out, how do you fix them?

On an upright piano, you can simply insert the needles of your upright voicing tool into the top of the problematic hammer a few times (Figure 27.2).

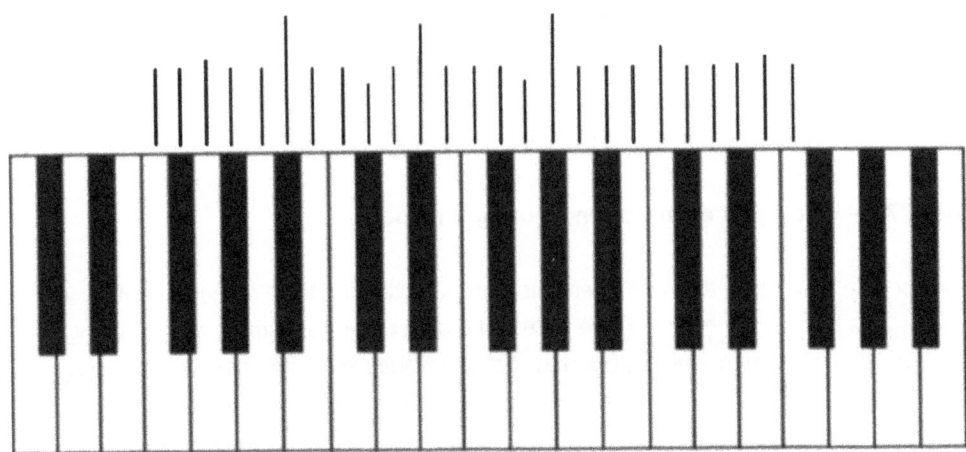

Figure 27.1 *Notice the longer lines on A♯, D♯, and G♯. These notes "stick out" from the others.*

On a grand piano, you will use what is called a chopstick needling tool. First secure the hammer using the following procedure:

1. Put the hammer in check.
2. Insert your chopstick tool in between the strings and use it to slide the hammer down the backcheck.
3. Lift up on the key ever so slightly and then press the key down hard.

The hammer is now locked in place. You can now insert the needle of your tool into the hammer. Insert it at an angle so that the needle goes into the hammer at the bottom of the string grooves and continues into the felt toward the center of the hammer (Figure 27.3). Video 27.1 shows how this is done.

Figure 27.2 *Upright voicing tool.*

🎵 **Video 27.1—How to insert the chopstick voicing tool.**

Now that we know what we are listening for and how to use the tools, let's watch Videos 27.2 and 27.3. In each, I will play a chromatic scale up and down with the same amount of force. See if you can hear the notes that stick out or sound accented.

In Video 27.2, there is one obvious "boulder" that sticks out. Can you hear it? Once that note is addressed, can you hear a few "rocks" that stick out slightly?

🎵 **Video 27.2—Voicing for evenness on a grand piano.**

Figure 27.3 *How to insert the chopstick voicing tool once the hammer is secure.*

Video 27.3 depicts how to address a handful of notes that stick out on an upright piano. Whenever I finish tuning a piano, I like to spend a few minutes voicing for evenness. I would encourage you to do the same.

🎵 **Video 27.3—Voicing for evenness on an upright piano.**

Some people worry that they will overdo it and make the note too soft. Fortunately, you can usually add a little power back into the note by holding down the strings with your finger (or a mute) and then striking the key to pound the hammers against the strings a few times. Video 27.4 shows this on a grand piano. The same technique can be used on an upright piano.

🎵 **Video 27.4—Adding some power back into the note.**

Two words of caution before we conclude.

First, avoid hyper-focusing on one area of the piano. If you aren't careful, you can find yourself going down a rabbit hole and voicing every note in one section so far that those notes no longer fit within the big picture of the rest of the piano's tone. To avoid this, periodically play outside of the smaller range of notes where you are working. Taking breaks to refresh your ears helps too.

Second, if you are a trained pianist, then you would think that you are at an advantage here. Shouldn't you of all people be able to play a chromatic scale with the same amount of force on each note? You'd think so; however, a trained pianist's subconscious mind will often compensate for a problem note by playing it with less force.

The pianist plays the scale, and one note sounds accented. But when they come back to that note again it sounds perfectly fine. The pianist doesn't even realize that they played it differently. Their brain is so used to making these adjustments during a performance. Playing the notes with two fingers (like you would when tuning) can help to overcome this natural tendency.

There is a lot more that goes into voicing a piano but learning to voice for evenness is fairly easy to learn and practice. It also happens to be one of the best things you can do to improve the tone of the pianos you will service.

Hands-on Homework: *Play a chromatic scale up and down on your practice piano. Try your best to strike each key with the same amount of force each time. See if you can find three or four notes that stick out. Voice those notes with your voicing tool until they more closely match the tone of their neighbors.*

For bonus points, do this assignment on both your upright and your grand practice pianos.

UNIT 6

Repairs

Tools You Will Need

Tools for Basic Repairs:

- Crescent wrench (x2)
- Screwdriver (flathead and Phillips)
- Flange screwdrivers (flathead and Phillips)
- Combination handle
- Magnetic retrieval tool
- Grand hammer head extractor
- Upright hammer head extractor
- Brass wire brush
- Key easing pliers
- Protek CLP
- Hypo oiler with a long needle
- Spare felt pieces
- Elmer's glue

Tools for String Replacement:

- Tuning lever
- String (various sizes)
- Needle-nose pliers
- Micrometer
- Dummy pin
- Coil maker
- Tuning pin crank
- Flat-nose pliers
- Music wire cutters
- Coil lifter
- Brass rod
- Hammer
- Screwdriver

A Few Notes on this Unit

Can you believe that we are on the last unit? How long has it taken you to arrive at this point?

I suppose you probably could have read this entire book within a few hours if you really wanted to, but I really hope you didn't. Stopping to take on the challenges of the Hands-on Homework assignments is infinitely more valuable to your learning and retention than reading alone could ever be.

I hope that you have been immersing yourself in this material for weeks (if not months) by the time you read this unit.

My goal in this unit is not to teach you everything. There are countless reasons why a note might click, or a key might stick. At this point in your education, a comprehensive list (if such a list could even be written) would feel daunting and overwhelming. My goal is to provide you with the top two or three reasons why each issue might arise, together with simple steps for addressing them.

There will be no Hands-on Homework in this unit, nor will there be a Unit Exam. Think of this last unit as a reference guide. Don't worry about internalizing everything you read, or even purchasing every tool. Instead, as you encounter these issues in the field, consult this unit and determine the source and the solution. Then purchase the tools needed to perform the task.

This might feel unprofessional, but when you are first starting out, most clients are more than happy to hear you say, "I've never come across this particular issue before, but I'd love to use the money from the tuning today to purchase the tools I need to come back and fix it. Is that alright?"

Now, let's explore some basic piano repairs.

28 Pedal Adjustments

While there are so many reasons the pedals might stop working, let's focus on two of the most common.

Lost Motion

The pedals should perform their functions not long after being depressed. Many pedals only start to perform their functions after the pedal has been depressed halfway through its travel (sometime not until the pedal has nearly finished its travel). This is particularly noticeable in the right and left pedals.

The right pedal should move only slightly before it starts to lift the dampers.

The left pedal on a grand piano should start to shift the action right when the pedal is pressed.

The left pedal on an upright piano should move only slightly before it starts to move the hammers closer to the strings.

Figure 28.1 *Pedal nuts for adjusting pedal lost motion in a grand piano.*

This adjustment is made on a grand piano by loosening the nuts on the top of the pedal rods (Figure 28.1), moving them up or down as needed, and then tightening them again with two crescent wrenches. Tightening with your fingers is usually not enough to ensure that the nuts will stay in place.

Some older pianos do not have an adjustment nut on the top of the pedal rods. If you need to adjust those pedal rods, then you can insert a piece of felt between the top of the pedal rod and the pedal mechanism.

On an upright piano this adjustment is made by turning the nuts indicated in Figure 28.2. Sometimes the nut turns the entire threaded rod underneath the pedal. If this happens, then you will likely need to hold the threaded rod with pliers while turning the adjustment nut with a wrench or your fingers.

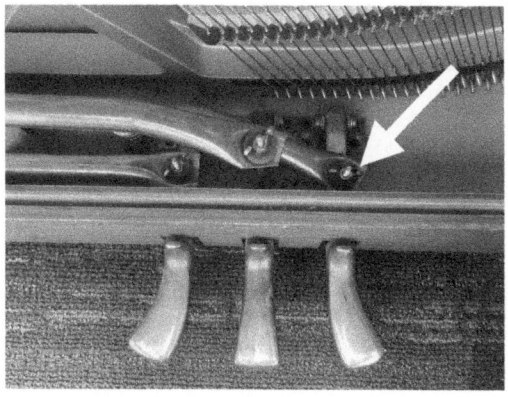

Figure 28.2 *Nuts for adjusting pedal lost motion in an upright piano pedal.*

Don't remove all lost motion on the right pedal (sustain pedal). If you do, then you risk the dampers ringing slightly. There should be just enough lost motion that the dampers don't ring.

Grand Action Shifting Too Far

The left pedal on a grand piano shifts the action toward the treble (to the right). The pedal should shift the hammer just far enough to barely miss (or just barely strike) the left string of each unison. If the hammers shift too far, then they risk striking the strings of the notes above them (see Video 28.1).

♪ **Video 28.1—Left pedal shifting a grand action too far.**

The solution is easy. There is a stop screw on the side of the treble cheekblock (Figure 28.3), or sometimes inside the piano on the treble side (Figure 28.4). Use a screwdriver to turn the screw out until the action shifts correctly. Be sure to screw in the cheekblock before making your final assessment.

Figure 28.3 *The stop screw on the side of the treble cheekblock.*

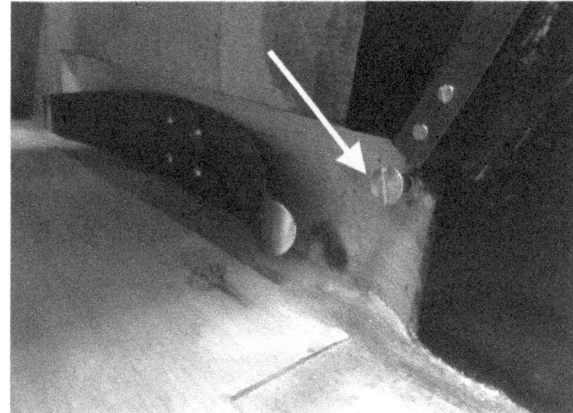

Figure 28.4 *The stop screw on the treble side of the inside of the piano.*

29 Clicks

In my experience, there are three common reasons for a piano action to make a clicking sound:

1. An object has fallen into the piano.
2. An action screw is loose.
3. A hammer head is loose.

An Object Has Fallen into the Piano

This one is pretty obvious, but it is still worth mentioning. Before you jump to any wild conclusions, be sure to remove the case parts and check for pencils, paper clips, or anything else that might have fallen inside of the piano action (Figure 29.1).

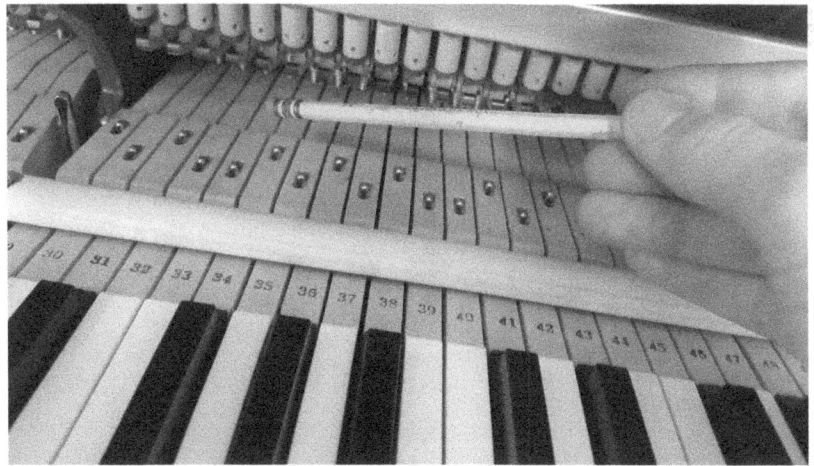

Figure 29.1 *Remove any object that has fallen into the piano.*

An Action Screw Is Loose

The two most common culprits are the screw for the hammer assembly and the screw for the wippen assembly.

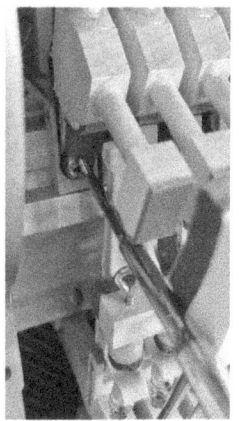

Figure 29.2 *A flange screwdriver tightening an upright hammer screw.*

If the click occurs when the hammer strikes the strings, then it is likely to be the screw for the hammer. In a grand piano, you can access the hammer screws by pulling the action onto your lap. In an upright, you will need to use a tool called a flange screwdriver. This tool is narrow and long enough to reach the screws (Figure 29.2). Often, it is attached to a combination handle.

If the click occurs when the key is released and the hammer falls back down, then it is more likely to be the screw for the wippen. In both an upright and grand piano, you will need to pull the action to access the wippen screws.

There is one other probable source of clicking to be aware of in a grand piano. If all the notes in large sections of the piano click when the keys are released and the hammers fall back down, then it is likely the result of a loose hammer rest rail. While your first reaction might be to pull the action and tighten the nut on top of the rest rail, always make sure to check that the nut underneath the hammer rest rail hasn't fallen down (Figure 29.3). If it has, then first turn the bottom nut up with your fingers, then tighten the top one with a screwdriver (Figure 29.4).

Figure 29.3 *The bottom nut needs to be raised first. Also, while unrelated to the issue at hand, notice that the wippens on this piano are black because they are made from a composite material.*

Figure 29.4 *Tightening the top nut.*

A Hammer Head Is Loose

The hammer head is glued to a long piece of wood called the hammer shank. Over time the hammer head can become loose and start to click when the hammer strikes the strings. You can usually feel that the hammer head is loose if you rock it back and forth with your fingers (Figure 29.5).

Once you've confirmed that the hammer head is loose, you will need to remove the hammer head and reglue it. Removing the hammer assembly is pretty straight forward on a grand piano. Simply pull the action onto your lap and unscrew the hammer assembly.

In an upright piano, removing the hammer is more difficult. Start by disconnecting the bridle strap. This is usually a red tab that attaches the hammer assembly to the wippen. Many people struggle with this at first. They have a particularly hard time getting it back on. Video 29.1 shows me removing and returning the bridle strap.

♪ **Video 29.1—Removing and returning the bridle strap.**

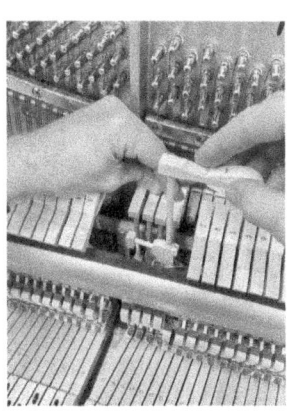

Figure 29.5 *Rocking the hammer head to feel if it's loose.*

Once the bridle strap is removed, you will need to use a flange screwdriver to unscrew the hammer screw. Be careful not to let the screw fall into the action. If it does fall, then a long magnetic retrieval tool can be used to fish it out.

Push the neighboring hammers forward with one hand, then rotate the hammer you are removing 90-degrees and pull it out (Figure 29.6)

You can now remove the hammer head from the hammer shank. This is done with a hammer head extractor. There are two types, one for grands (Figure 29.7) and one for uprights (Figure 29.8). Sometimes you may need to heat up the glue joint with a lighter or a heat gun to remove the hammer heads, but since these hammers were so loose they were clicking, they should pop off without any heat. In fact, sometimes the hammer is so loose that you can pop it off with your fingers.

Figure 29.6 *Removing an upright hammer assembly.*

Once the hammer is removed, return the hammer shank to the piano. In a grand, this simply means screwing it back in. In an upright, you will need to push the neighboring hammers out of the way. Insert the hammer shank and hammer butt parallel to the hammer rest rail, then rotate them 90-degrees. Being careful not to let the screw fall out, align the screw to the hole and use a flange screwdriver to tighten the screw. This can be an incredibly frustrating process, especially the first few times you do it. Finally, return the bridle strap to the bridle

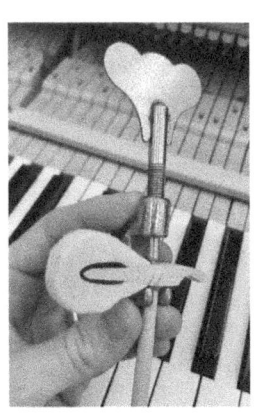

Figure 29.7 *Grand hammer head extractor.*

Figure 29.8 *Upright hammer head extractor.*

wire. When doing this, you may need to pull the jack forward toward you (away from the hammer butt) to get enough slack in the bridle strap. If it's too taught, don't try to force it. Identify what's causing the hang up first.

You can now put a little Elmer's glue around the top of the hammer shank and glue the hammer head back onto the hammer shank. Before the glue dries, be sure to match the angle of the hammer with its neighbors. Also, ensure that the top of the hammer is in the same plane as its neighbors and then align the string grooves on the hammer to the strings.

Since there is a lot going on here, Video 29.2 shows this entire process from start to finish on a grand piano. Video 29.3 shows this repair on an upright piano.

♪ **Video 29.2—Regluing a loose hammer head to the hammer shank on a grand piano.**

♪ **Video 29.3—Regluing a loose hammer head to the hammer shank on an upright piano.**

30 Buzzes and Rattles

The top two reasons for a buzz or a rattle in a piano are:

1. An object has fallen into the piano.
2. A case screw is loose.

Notice how similar these two reasons are to the first two reasons for a click in the piano. While not a hard and fast rule, the following tends to be true:

When an object falls into the piano action it clicks. When an object falls onto the soundboard, it buzzes or rattles.

When an action screw is loose, it clicks. When a case screw is loose, it buzzes or rattles.

An Object Has Fallen into the Piano

Conceptually, this is straightforward. The hardest part is finding the object, especially because it may be hidden under the cast-iron plate. A can of compressed air and a long magnetic retrieval tool can be helpful (Figure 30.1).

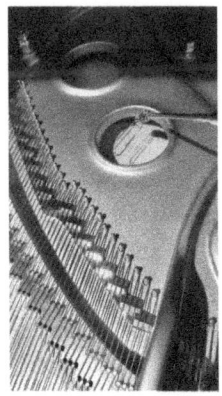

Figure 30.1 *Retrieving an object from off the soundboard.*

A Case Screw Is Loose

These include the screws in the lid, the screws where the lid locator pin is inserted (Figure 30.2), and while not a screw, the lid hinge pins. In this last case, you may need to remove the lid hinge pin and bend it slightly before reinserting it.

Another screw (or nut) that can rattle is found on the key stop rail (Figure 30.3). These ones are a little trickier to find since they require removing the fallboard. This is an exception to the rule of thumb mentioned earlier that clicks usually come from the action and buzzes usually come from the soundboard.

Figure 30.2 *Tightening a case screw.*

Figure 30.3 *The nuts on the key stop rail can also rattle if they become loose.*

By far the most difficult part is finding the source of the rattle or buzz. When looking for a buzz, play the note repeatedly with one hand while pressing your other hand on any surface you suspect might be the cause. If the buzz stops, then you know that you have found the source. Remember that sometimes a buzz can come from an object outside the piano, such as a lamp, a picture frame, or a snare drum on a drum set.

31 Squeaks

There are two common places for squeaks: the pedals and the action.

In the action, a squeak usually occurs when:

1 Friction builds up between one of the action contact points.

In the pedals, a squeak can occur when:

1 Friction builds up at one of the pedal contact points.
2 Friction builds up between the action and the keybed when shifting (grand pianos only).
3 The pedal lyre is loose (grand pianos only).

Friction in the Action Contact Points

These squeaks can occur at the balance rail pin, between the capstan and the wippen, between the repetition spring and the underside of the repetition lever, and between the top of the jack and the hammer knuckle. These squeaks (or creaks) are often best heard during a slow keystroke that doesn't strike the strings.

The solution is usually as simple as applying a safe lubricant such as such as Protek CLP to the contact point in a hypo oiler (Figure 31.1). For the friction build up between the jack and the hammer knuckle, you can use a brass wire brush to brush the knuckle toward you (Figure 31.2).

Figure 31.1 *Lubricating the balance rail pin.*

Figure 31.2 *Brushing a hammer knuckle.*

Friction in the Pedal Contact Points

There are multiple contact points in the pedal systems of grand and upright pianos. Figures 31.3 and 31.4 show some common locations for pedal squeaks in the right pedal of a grand piano. Of these, only location #5 would require removing the action to access.

Figures 31.5, 31.6, 31.7, 31.8, and 31.9 show common locations for pedal squeaks in the right pedal of an upright piano. Of these, locations #4 and #5 would require removing the action to access.

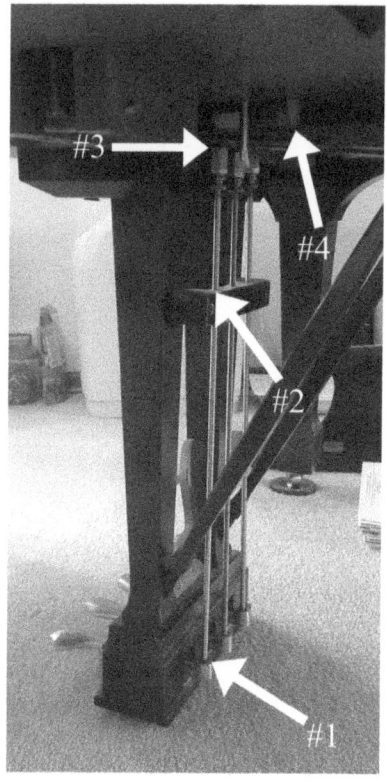

Figure 31.3 *Some common locations for pedal squeaks in a grand piano.*

Figure 31.4 *Some common locations for pedal squeaks in a grand piano.*

Once you identify the location of the squeak, lubricate it with Protek CLP or replace any worn felts or leather as needed.

While these locations are most common, they are not the only locations in which a squeak may occur. Do your best to isolate each part of the pedal system to properly identify the actual source of the squeak.

Friction between the Action and the Keybed When Shifting

This problem is unique to grand pianos. The action shifts toward the treble when the left pedal is pressed. A squeak can occur when there is too much friction between the action and the keybed (the wood on which the action rests).

To resolve this issue, remove the action, clean the keybed of any dust, and lubricate the contact areas where the action contacts the keybed with a safe lubricant, such as McLube. In particular, along the front and at the five or so locations where bolts in the middle of the action contact the keybed (see Figure 31.10).

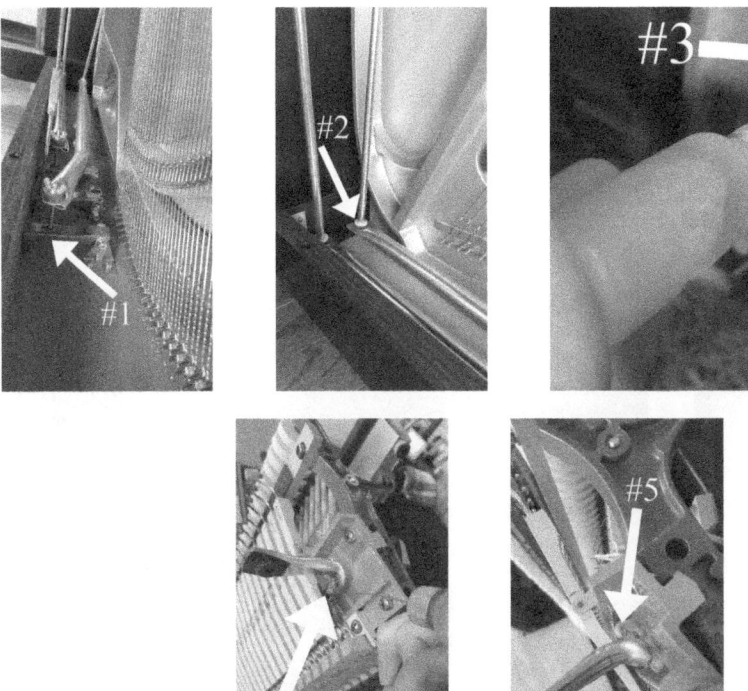

Figures 31.5–31.9 *Some common locations for pedal squeaks in an upright piano.*

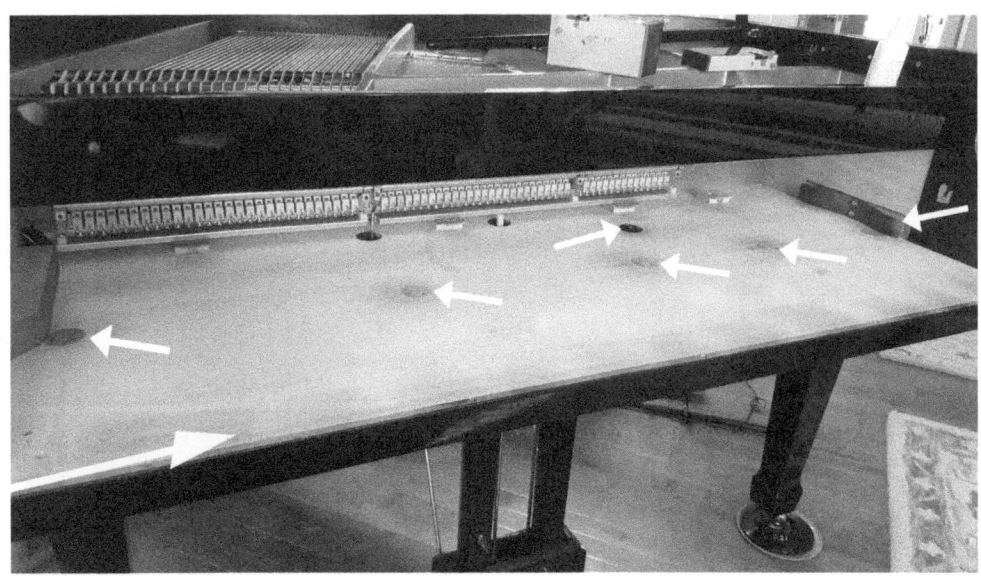

Figure 31.10 *Where to lubricate the keybed.*

Loose Pedal Lyre

On a grand piano, the pedals are attached to a piece of wood underneath the piano called the lyre. If the lyre is loose, then all three pedals can squeak. To address this issue, you need to tighten the bolts that hold the lyre in place (Figure 31.11). On some pianos, you can also tighten the screws in the support rods (Figure 31.12).

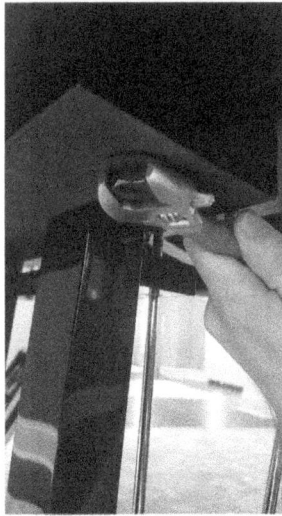

Figure 31.11 *Tightening the lyre.*

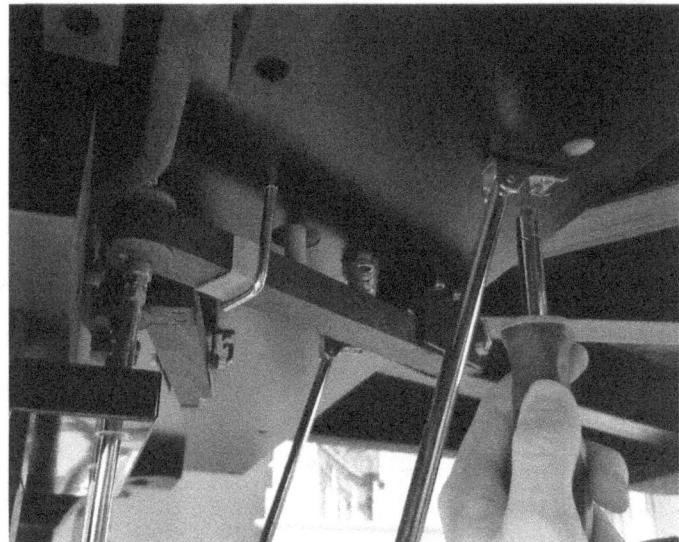

Figure 31.12 *Tightening the lyre supports.*

32 Double-Striking Hammers

When a piano isn't regulated correctly its hammers can double-strike. This means that the hammer hits the strings twice in quick succession (Video 32.1).

🎵 **Video 32.1—Examples of double-striking hammers.**

Double-Striking Hammers in an Upright Piano

If you come across double-striking hammers in an upright piano, start by removing any lost motion in the problematic notes. If this solves the issue, then it is well worth taking the time to remove the lost motion throughout the entire piano.

If this doesn't solve the issue, then you will need to increase the amount of aftertouch in the piano.

In Lesson 22, we learned that there are two main means of increasing aftertouch. We can either decrease the blow distance (move the hammers closer to the strings), or we can increase the key dip by removing front rail punchings.

Unfortunately, adjusting the blow distance and key dip (together with the chain-reaction adjustments that accompany them) takes a fair amount of time. For this reason, many technicians choose to use a technique called "shimming the balance rail."

The balance rail is the wooden rail that runs underneath the middle of the keys. The balance rail pins are attached to the balance rail. Adjusting the balance rail punchings adjusts the key height.

If the height of the key is higher, then there is more key dip. This is because key dip is measured as the distance from the starting point of the key to its location at the bottom of the key's travel. If the starting point of the key is higher, then that means that the key has more room to travel before bottoming out.

While we could increase the key height of a single note by adding a balance rail punching, on an upright piano, we can increase the key height of an entire section of notes by inserting business cards or thin cardboard punchings underneath the balance rail.

To do this, we must first locate the screws in the balance rail. Remove keys until you find them. Then loosen the screws and lift up on the balance rail. Insert the business cards or thin cardboard punchings underneath the balance rail and tighten the screws (Figure 32.1). This will raise the balance rail, which raises the key height. This also increases the key travel, which increases the amount of aftertouch.

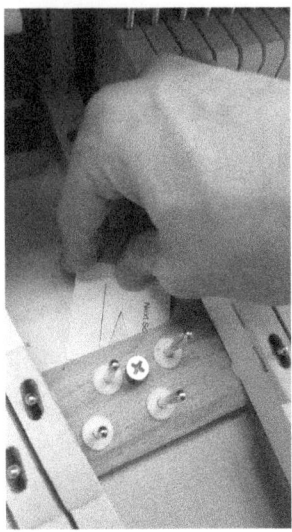

Figure 32.1 *Putting a business card underneath the balance rail.*

In theory, you should now go back and reset the checking distances throughout the piano, but this is almost never done when shimming the balance rail to address double-striking hammers. There is no doubt that the piano needs to be regulated, but the immediate problem is solved and so most people leave it at that.

Double-Striking Hammers in a Grand Piano

Double-striking hammers can also occur in a grand piano. Unfortunately, the solution isn't as straightforward. Often, adjusting the checking distance and weakening the spring tension will help. It is more likely there are friction issues related to loose center pins, but that is beyond the scope of this book. For now, just do your best to adjust the checking and spring tension until the hammer stops double-striking.

33 Sticky Keys

These are the top three reasons for a sticky key:

1   A natural key is rubbing against the keyslip.
2   A key bushing is too tight.
3   A center pin is too tight.

A Natural Key Is Rubbing Against the Keyslip

The keyslip is the piece of wood that runs directly in front of the keys. Over time, the keyslip can warp and move closer to the keys. When this happens, natural keys (white keys) can rub against the keyslip and stick. A telltale sign of this problem is that only one natural key will stick at a time. This is because the depressed key will push the keyslip far enough away for the other keys to move freely.

How do you fix it? First, remove the keyslip. Depending on the piano you may need to remove the cheekblocks first. Some pianos have a screw you can adjust on the front of the cheekblock. If so, simply unscrew it slightly and you're done, just make sure it isn't so loose that the keyslip flops around. If there isn't a screw, then you can place a shim (for example, a piece of business card) between the keyslip and the cheekblocks or keyframe as needed (Figure 33.1). This moves the keyslip away from the keys and allows them to move freely.

A Key Bushing Is Too Tight

Underneath the front of the key there is a cloth bushing. This bushing allows the key to move up and down smoothly on the front rail pin (sometimes called bat pins in the UK). If a key bushing is too tight, then it will bind on the front rail pin and the key will stick down. You can diagnose this by lifting the hammer up to see if it falls back down freely. If the hammer falls without resistance, then there is a good chance there is too much friction between the front rail pin and the bushing at the front of the key.

To solve this problem, remove the key stop rail and lift the key up until you can access the bushings with key easing pliers. There are two types of key easing pliers. In Figure 33.2, the pliers on the right require you to remove the key to use them. In a grand piano, this means removing

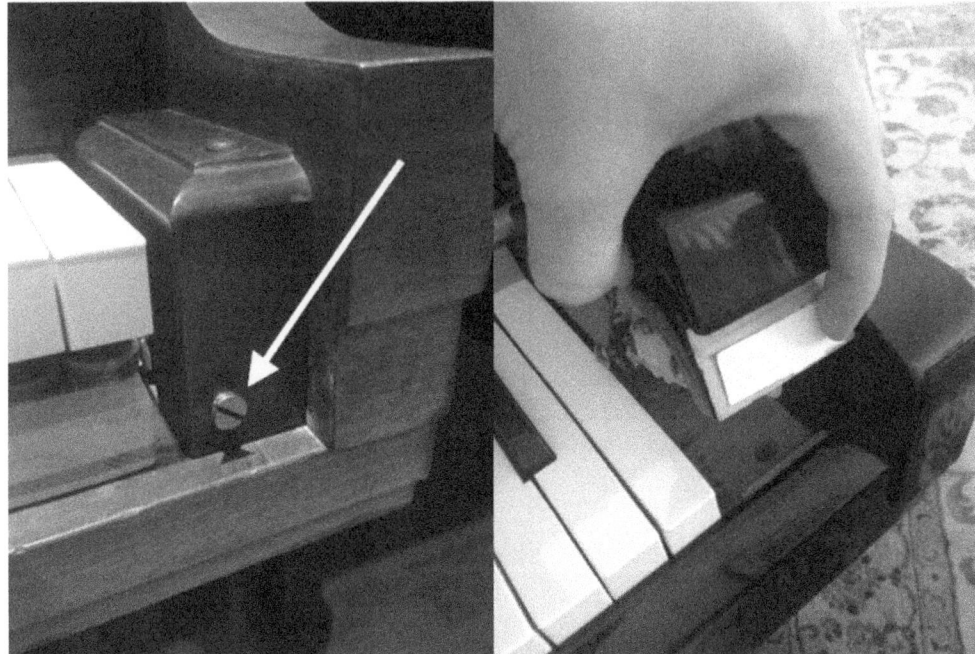

Figure 33.1 *Moving the keyslip farther away from the keys.*

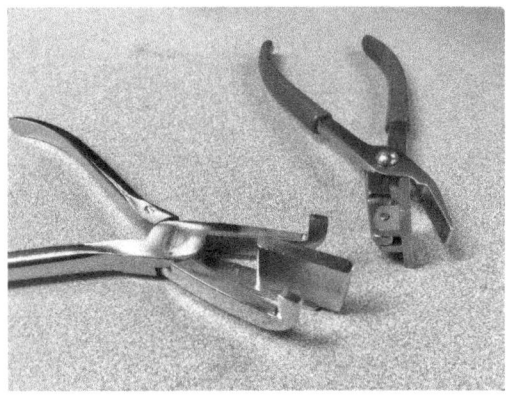

Figure 33.2 *Key easing pliers.*

the action stack. The pliers on the left can be used with the action stack on.

Once you have the pliers in place, gently compress the cloth bushing on both sides (Figure 33.3). Pressing too hard may crack the wood of the key and make the key too loose. Think of it like a firm handshake. You don't want to "dead fish" the key, but you don't want to "hulk smash" the wood either.

Once finished, return the key, and see if it moves up and down freely. Then move the key side to side. There should be a slight clicking feeling (not sound) in both directions. If a small amount of side play isn't present, then you may need to ease a little more.

A Center Pin Is Too Tight

At each rotation point in the action there is a tiny pin (Figure 33.4). If that pin becomes tight inside the cloth bushing, then the action parts will seize up and stick. In this case, it isn't actually the key that is sticking, but this is how a pianist will most likely describe it. Whenever someone tells me that they have a sticky key on their piano, I always ask, "Is the key visually sticking down?" I am surprised by how often the answer is "No."

The most common offender tends to be the pin on which the hammer rotates. You can confirm this by pulling the action onto your lap, lifting the hammer up, and letting it go. Does the hammer fall back down? Or does it stay up as it does in Video 33.1? Or does it fall more slowly than its neighbors?

♪ **Video 33.1—Tight hammer pin. Notice how the hammer doesn't fall back down when lifted.**

The pin in the hammer isn't the only one that can get tight. If the pin in the jack is too tight, then the hammer will strike once but will not repeat. This one is easy to diagnose. Just listen for descriptions like: "It's so strange! The note will play once, but it won't play again!"

The correct solution to these issues is to remove the pin, ease the cloth bushing, and then insert a new pin of the correct size. This process is called "repinning" ("recentering" in the UK). While not terribly difficult, the repinning procedure is nuanced and requires several specialized tools and supplies. As a result, I will instead recommend applying some Protek CLP to the problematic center pin. While not necessarily a permanent fix, it should resolve the immediate issue. Just be sure to add repinning to your list of skills to learn from a mentor.

Figure 33.3 *Easing the key bushing.*

Figure 33.4 *Center pins in the grand piano action.*

34 Ringing Dampers

If a grand piano was moved recently, then the pitman that presses up on the tray that lifts the dampers can become dislodged (Figure 34.1). This is a common reason for ringing dampers. Fortunately, the solution is straightforward, if you know how to pull the action—which you do! To resolve this issue, pull the action out completely and insert the pitman back into its place.

In Lesson 28 I mentioned that if you remove all the lost motion in the right pedal, then you risk the dampers being lifted slightly off the strings. To test for this, use a mute to push down on the strings slightly. The damper should follow the strings. If it doesn't, then you know that you need to introduce a little more lost motion to the right pedal. See Video 34.1.

Figure 34.1 *Pitman is dislodged.*

♪ **Video 34.1—Dampers should follow the strings when they are pressed down.**

Another common damper issue is what I call a "leaky" damper. This problem is often found in the tri-chord wedge dampers. Sometimes the felt isn't in proper contact with either the right or the left string in a unison. You can test for this by inserting a mute on the right and left strings and listening to how well the note dampens. If the left string is leaking slightly, then you can insert a small screwdriver into the felt and push upward and diagonally to the left (Figure 34.2). This will move the felt over slightly to help it make better contact with the left string (see Video 34.2).

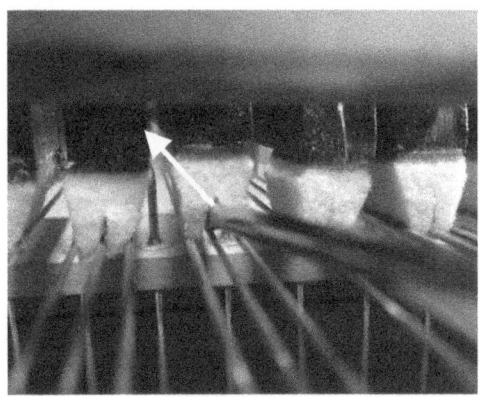

Figure 34.2 *Insert a small screwdriver into the felt and push upward and diagonally in the direction of the leaky string.*

♪ **Video 34.2—Fixing a leaky damper.**

If the right string is leaking, then you would simply push upward and to the right. Keep in mind that some dampers have tri-chord wedges on both the front and the back of the damper head. Often you will need to push the felts on both sides of the damper head to get the desired result.

There are plenty of other reasons why a damper might ring or leak, but an in-depth look at damper work will also have to wait for another time.

35 Broken Strings

I'll be honest. I didn't want to include this lesson. Replacing a broken string is a more complex repair. It is full of small but critical steps, each requiring the use of specialized tools and an understanding of specific terminology. It is also difficult to practice without access to a jig, or a piano on which you are allowed to break strings.

In the end, I realized that there really is no way around it. If a string breaks, then you will be expected to fix it. Whether it was already broken when you arrived, or if the string breaks while you are tuning.

Notice how I phrased the end of that last sentence. *You* did not break the string. The string broke while you were tuning. This is an important distinction. Strings typically break because they are older, or rusted, or corroded—none of which is your fault. If you see a piano with rusted strings, then you can tell the customer in advance that some strings may break if you tune the piano. For your part, you can put some CLP over the friction points on the string and be sure to push the strings slightly flat before pulling them sharp. This should help, but it is no guarantee.

Let's start by defining some terms.

String Replacement Terminology:

Tuning pin (Wrest pin in the UK)—The metal piece that holds the strings and is adjusted to tune the piano.

Agraffe—The metal piece that the strings run through after leaving the tuning pin. This establishes one end of the speaking length of the string. Agraffes are generally found in the bass and midrange of grand pianos.

V-bar, Capo bar, or Pressure bar—Three names for the metal piece that the string runs under after leaving the tuning pin. This establishes one end of the speaking length of the string when agraffes are not used.

Bridge pins—The two pins on the bridge through which the string runs. The bridge pin closest to the player establishes the other end of the speaking length of the string.

Aliquot—The metal piece that rests on the plate in front of the hitch pins. This establishes the length of the back duplex.

Hitch pin—The pin inserted into the plate. The string is bent around this pin before heading back across the aliquot, bridge pins, and back through the agraffe (or under the capo bar) before it is coiled around another tuning pin.

Becket—The section of the wire that goes through the tuning pin.

String Replacement Tools:

- Brass rod
- Coil lifter
- Coil maker
- Dummy tuning pin
- Flat-nose pliers
- Hammer
- Micrometer
- Music wire cutters
- Needle-nose pliers
- Screwdriver
- String (various sizes)
- Tuning lever
- Tuning pin crank

Read through the steps below, then watch the video at the end. When you've finished, go back and read the steps again, then watch the video again. It is a lot to work through in one sitting. You likely won't get a true sense for this repair until you can work through it a couple of times (preferably with a mentor).

In an upright piano you will need to remove the action to gain access to the bridge pins and hitch pins.

Step 1: Use your tuning lever to back the tuning pins out 1.25 turns (or 5 quarter turns). Use pliers to remove the old strings and coils. Cut the string as needed to remove it. Measure the old string with a micrometer.

Many pianos have the gauge of the strings stamped on the plate or the bridge; however, those numbers mean different things depending on whether the piano manufacturer used imperial or metric measurements. It is a good practice to measure replacement wire with a micrometer and ensure that it matches the original string gauge.

The formula for imperial strings is:

$$(\text{Micrometer Number} - 5) / 2 = \text{String Gauge}$$

For metric strings, add 0.5 to the string gauge you get from the formula above.
The conversions in Table 35.1 are useful.

Table 35.1 *String sizes*

US	Metric	Inches	Millimeters
12.5	13.0	0.0305	0.775
13.0	13.5	0.0315	0.800
13.5	14.0	0.0325	0.825
14.0	14.5	0.0335	0.850
14.5	15.0	0.0344	0.875
15.0	15.5	0.0354	0.900
15.5	16.0	0.0364	0.925
16.0	16.5	0.0374	0.950
16.5	17.0	0.0384	0.975
17.0	17.5	0.0394	1.000
17.5	18.0	0.0404	1.025
18.0	18.5	0.0413	1.050

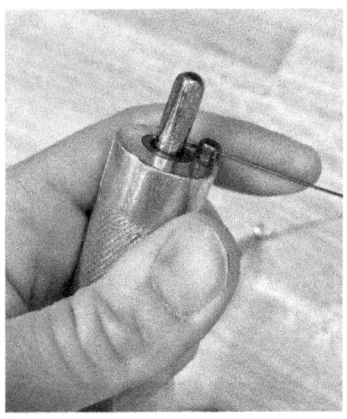

Figure 35.1 *How to hold everything when making a coil on the dummy pin. Notice how my index finger is pushing the string into the stop screw on the coil maker. The string is just barely poking out of the back end of the hole in the dummy tuning pin.*

Step 2: Take the appropriately sized string and run it through the agraffe or under the capo bar.

Step 3: Use a dummy pin, a coil maker, and a tuning pin crank to make a coil. Make sure the string is through the pin and just barely visible in the hole. Use your index finger to apply pressure to the string in the coil maker (see Figure 35.1), then turn the dummy pin 2½ times with the tuning pin crank. The first bend is the most important.

This step can be tricky at first. You might want to make several practice coils before trying the entire string replacement process.

Step 4: Use needle-nose pliers to remove the coil from the dummy pin and place it on the pin in the piano (Figure 35.2). It helps to grab the becket with the pliers and pry it out by applying pressure to the top of the dummy pin.

Step 5: Insert the becket into the small hole in the pin and use flat-nose pliers to push it all the way through. Use your tuning lever to give the pin a slight turn. Then squeeze the becket again to make sure it stays in place.

Step 6: Run the string through the bridge pins and put a nice bend in the string by pulling it hard around the hitch pin.

Step 7: Run the string through the bridge pins, then pull the string tight and cut it just above the back of the key tops. Then run this end of the wire through the agraffe (or under the capo bar) and pull it tight. Use your wire cutters to cut the string about a four-finger distance when your thumb and index finger are directly over the pin where the string will be placed (Figure 35.3). Throw the excess wire away.

Step 8: Repeat Steps 3 to 5 on this end of the string.

Step 9: Make sure the strings are running through the bridge pins and then use your tuning lever to tighten the strings while simultaneously pulling up on the coil with a coil lifter. As you tighten, make sure the string moves up onto the aliquot. Also, be sure to stop periodically to tighten the becket with flat-nose pliers.

Step 10: Make adjustments as needed until all of the requirements listed below are met:

Figure 35.2 *Prying the string off the dummy pin.*

- The coils should be at the appropriate height on the pin. Which is, when the coil covers about ½ of the hole on the opposite side of the pin from the becket. If the coil is too high, then tap it down with a brass rod and a hammer. If the coil is too low, then loosen the tuning pin slightly with your tuning lever. Use the coil lifter to lift the coil up, and then tighten the tuning pin again.
- The coils should be tight. You can use a hammer and brass rod to tap them down, if needed.
- The becket should be tight in the pin. Use flat-nose pliers to squeeze the becket in as much as you can.
- The string should be fully seated at the base of the hitch pin. Use a brass rod to tap it down, if needed.
- The strings should be aligned to the grooves in the hammer when in the V-bar section. Use a flathead screwdriver to push the strings side to side until they are aligned.

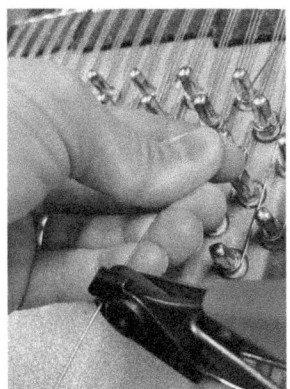

Figure 35.3 *With your index finger and thumb over the pin, cut the string at a four-finger width distance.*

Step 11: Seat the strings to the bridge by tapping them lightly with a brass rod. Tap in the direction of the bridge pins.

Step 12: Pull the strings up to pitch, then put your finger on the strings and play the key hard a few times. This will cause the pitch to slip. Pull the strings up to pitch again and play the key with your finger on the strings. Repeat as needed until the pitch doesn't slip when played. The strings will still go out of tune quickly. Be sure to schedule a return visit to touch up the tuning on the replacement strings within a week or so after the repair. I include this return visit in the cost of this repair. Video 35.1 shows the entire string replacement process.

♪ **Video 35.1—The string replacement process.**

Final Exam

This final exam includes questions relating to everything we have covered together over the last thirty-five lessons. Do your best to answer these questions without referencing the book. Instead, take the test in front of a piano and reason through the questions by examining the instrument itself. The answers can be found in the answer key at the end of this book.

Congratulations! You have finished this introduction to piano technology! While you might not be able to go out and make a living servicing pianos just yet, you now have a much clearer idea of the skills and tools you would need to do so.

There is still so much more to learn. By completing your final exam, you have demonstrated how much you know. Equally as important is knowing what you *do not* know.

Below is a list of some important topics we did not cover in this book. Start working through the topics on this list with a mentor as soon as you can.

- Aural tuning
- Servicing grand and upright dampers
- Using an aftertouch gauge to achieve consistent aftertouch throughout the keyboard
- Achieving simultaneous escapement on a grand piano
- Adjusting upright bridle wires
- Bedding the keyframe of a grand piano
- Hammer traveling
- Alignment of action parts
- How to determine an appropriate key height
- Key leveling, aligning, and squaring
- Hammer filing
- Hammer mating
- Key rebushing
- Flange rebushing
- Repinning
- Hitch pin loops
- String splicing
- Bass string replacement
- Grand hammer shank replacement
- Vertical hammer shank replacement
- Sostenuto adjustment

The learning doesn't stop there either! Once you've conquered the items on the list above, you can begin to explore everything that goes into piano rebuilding. One of the things I love most about this craft is that there is always more to learn and explore.

Final Exam

1. Put the four types of uprights into the correct order from smallest to largest.
2. True or False:

   The only type of upright still being manufactured today is the studio upright.
3. What size grand piano is known as a "baby grand"?

   a Under 5 feet

   b Under 6 feet

   c Under 6.5 feet

   d There is no formal definition
4. True or False:

   You need to remove the action to tune an upright piano.
5. True or False:

   You need to remove the action to tune a grand piano.
6. When removing an upright piano action, which of the following action components stays inside the piano?

   a Dampers

   b Wippens

   c Keys

   d Hammers
7. When removing a grand piano action, which of the following action components stays inside the piano?

   a Dampers

   b Wippens

   c Keys

   d Hammers
8. The damper spoons on an upright piano are located on the …

   a keys

   b hammers

   c wippens

   d dampers

9 The backchecks on an upright piano are located on the …

   a keys
   b hammers
   c wippens
   d dampers

10 The backcheck on a grand is located on the …

   a keys
   b hammers
   c wippens
   d dampers

11 The damper on a grand piano is lifted by the …

   a damper spoon
   b back of the key
   c capstan
   d repetition Lever

12 True or False:

   The best way to clean dust from off the soundboard of a grand piano is with a vacuum.

13 In an upright piano, the capstan adjusts the …

   a key dip
   b blow distance
   c key height
   d lost motion

14 In a grand piano, the capstan adjusts the …

   a key dip
   b blow distance
   c key height
   d lost motion

15 In both an upright and grand piano, escapement begins when these two action parts touch. Select the two that apply:
- **a** The jack toe
- **b** The wippen
- **c** The capstan
- **d** The let-off button
- **e** The backcheck
- **f** The damper

16 At what speed do you need to play the key to measure the let-off?
- **a** With a medium blow
- **b** Very slowly
- **c** Very quickly

17 At what speed do you need to play the key to measure the checking?
- **a** With a medium blow
- **b** Very slowly
- **c** Very quickly

18 At which of these measurements is the hammer closest to the strings?
- **a** Blow distance
- **b** Drop
- **c** Let-off
- **d** Checking

19 If you press and hold a key, the hammer will be …
- **a** in check
- **b** at the point of let-off
- **c** in contact with the string
- **d** voiced for evenness

20 Which of the following is a good ballpark range for key dip?
- **a** 2 millimeters
- **b** 8 millimeters
- **c** 10 millimeters
- **d** 15 millimeters

21 Which of the following is a good ballpark range for let-off?

- **a** 2 millimeters
- **b** 8 millimeters
- **c** 10 millimeters
- **d** 15 millimeters

22 Which of the following is a good ballpark range for checking?

- **a** 2 millimeters
- **b** 8 millimeters
- **c** 10 millimeters
- **d** 15 millimeters

23 True or False:

In an upright piano, the hammers should rest on the hammer rest rail.

24 True or False:

In a grand piano, the hammers should rest on the hammer rest rail or rest cushions.

25 True or False:

In an upright piano, the blow distance can be adjusted for an individual hammer.

26 True or False:

In a grand piano, the blow distance can be adjusted for an individual hammer.

27 In an upright piano, when blow distance is adjusted, what two things need to be reset?

- **a** Lost motion and checking
- **b** Lost motion and key dip
- **c** Let-off and key dip
- **d** Let-off and checking

28 In an upright piano, when key dip is adjusted, what needs to be reset?

- **a** Let-off
- **b** Checking
- **c** Lost motion
- **d** Key height

29 Put the following moments of a slow keystroke in order:

- The hammer rises from its at-rest position
- Aftertouch rise
- Drop
- Let-off

30 The three adjustments on the grand wippen are _____, _____, and _____?

31 When you put the hammer of a grand piano in check, then let up on the key slightly, the hammer should …

    a play the strings again

    b fall back down slowly

    c rise quickly without bobbling at the top

    d rise quickly with a bobble at the top

32 Which of the following will increase aftertouch. Select all that apply:

    a Increase the key dip

    b Decrease the key dip

    c Increase the blow distance (move the hammers farther away from the strings)

    d Decrease the blow distance (move the hammers closer to the strings)

33 True or False:

If the hammers on an upright piano are double-striking, then the piano likely has too much aftertouch.

34 True or False:

If the hammer shanks of a grand piano are on the rest rail (or rest cushions), then the piano likely has too much aftertouch.

35 True or False:

Tuning with your tuning lever in line with the strings will usually give you more control.

36 True or False:

If a unison is pure (meaning without beats) it doesn't matter if the bottom of the tuning pin didn't move when it was tuned.

37 Put the following steps in the correct order for a typical unison tuning:

- Refine with the z-axis
- Test for stability
- Click up
- Nudge down

38 True or False:

A piano that is 20 cents flat will need a pitch raise.

39 True or False:

Each piano is tuned to a custom tuning.

40 When voicing for evenness, you are listening for notes that …

   a are out of tune

   b stick out or sound accented

   c click

   d don't play

41 True or False:

The right pedal should have absolutely no lost motion.

42 When you press the left pedal on a grand piano, the hammers should …

   a rise toward the strings

   b shift to play the neighboring notes

   c shift to just barely miss (or just barely play) the left string

   d raise the dampers

43 Clicks are usually the result of something that is loose …

   a on the soundboard or in the case of the piano

   b in the action of the piano

44 Buzzes are usually the result of something that is loose …

   a on the soundboard or in the case of the piano

   b in the action of the piano

45 True or False:

Squeaks occur when friction builds up in the action or the pedals.

46 What are two things you could do to address double-striking hammers in a grand piano? Select the two that apply:

   a Strengthen the repetition spring

   b Weaken the repetition spring

   c Adjust the checking distance

   d Shim the balance rail

47 Which of the following is NOT one of the reasons a key might stick?

   a A tight key bushing

   b A tight center pin

   c A tight hammer shank

   d A key is rubbing on the keyslip

48 If the dampers are ringing after a grand piano has been moved, then it is likely that …

   a the movers put the legs back on incorrectly
   b the damper felts were damaged in the move
   c the fallboard was damaged in the move
   d the pitman for the damper tray fell out in the move

49 True or False:

Piano wires are all the same thickness.

50 True or False:

If a string breaks while you are tuning, then you are at fault.

Bonus Lesson Running a Business

Since I still have your attention, allow me to share one last lesson with you. My fear is that learning how to work on pianos can be so exciting that you may be tempted to overlook the more mundane realities of this career. Namely, building and running a profitable piano service business.

Many people feel the allure of becoming their own boss, but what they often fail to recognize is the responsibility it carries. Most full-time tuners service around four pianos per day, or close to 1,000 appointments per year. How do you generate that kind of business? How do you schedule all those appointments to minimize travel times? How do you manage all your customer and service records? And how do you decide how much time you should spend each day on these managerial and clerical tasks?

Another area where I see piano technicians struggle is in managing their finances. For example, let's say you charge $150 per tuning and are averaging three appointments per day. How much do you make?

Many people would say, "Well, $150 at 3 pianos a day … I make around $112,500 per year, minus a little for gas money I suppose."

If only it were so simple.

First of all, don't forget about taxes. These will likely come close to 20 percent of your business' income. What benefits would you like to have? Sick days? Paid vacations? Are you planning to retire someday?—The answer is yes by the way. What about health insurance for you and your family? You also need to carry liability insurance in case you damage someone's home or their piano. Is continuing education important to you?—It should be!

While that $122,500 might seem like a lot of money at first glance, the reality might look more like this chart. If you live outside of the United States, then you will have to convert these numbers into your own currency. Although, the specific numbers aren't really the focus here. The key takeaway is this:

Income—Expenses = What Your Business Actually Makes

Expense	Annual Cost	Deductions Per Tuning
Taxes (20%)	$22,050	$30.00
Profit for investment into your business (10%)	$11,025	$15.00
Retirement investments (15%)	$16,500	$22.50
Health insurance	$7,000	$9.50
Life insurance	$250	$0.35
Disability insurance	$550	$0.75
Liability insurance	$1,000	$1.40

Expense	Annual Cost	Deductions Per Tuning
Car insurance	$1,500	$2.00
Ten days of holiday pay	$4,500	$6.00
Ten vacation days	$4,500	$6.00
Five sick days	$2,250	$3.00
Professional dues and continuing education	$4,000	$5.50
Website and other marketing fees	$3,000	$4.00
Mileage, car maintenance, parking, and tolls	$6,000	$8.00
Miscellaneous expenses	$2,000	$3.00
Total expenses/deductions per tuning	**$86,125**	**$117.00**
Your salary/What you make per tuning	**$24,125**	**$33.00**

When all is said and done, you made closer to $24,000 with excellent benefits. To generate more income, you could raise your prices and/or tune more pianos. Of course, you could also sacrifice vacation days, your business' profit margin, or any of the other items listed in the chart to increase your take-home pay. Many technicians choose to do so (even if that decision was made without realizing it). Tragically, far too many piano tuners love what they do so much that they simply don't charge enough to be profitable, and as a result go uninsured, without paid vacations, and hardly, if ever, invest in retirement. Don't make this mistake. Realize that being your own boss is both a blessing and a burden. Don't quit your day job just because you read this book. Make the jump into this industry at the right time and in the right way.

Of course, not all piano technicians choose to be self-employed. Some choose to work for other technicians, for a piano dealership, or for a college or university. Personally, I work full-time for a university and tune privately on the side. Each option comes with its own pros and cons. Only you know what will work best for you and your family.

Conclusion What's the Next Step?

By now I hope you realize that this conclusion is actually just a new beginning. Where do you go from here? Well, I suppose that depends on your interest. Let's return to a variation of the question I asked in the introduction: On a scale of 1 to 10, how committed are you to making a living working on pianos?

Perhaps you've realized that this career path isn't for you. That's completely fine! I'm so glad you will never have to lose sleep wondering, "but what if … ?" Although, if you made it this far, then I doubt you fall into this category.

Perhaps you see this as a nice side-hustle, at least for now. If it evolves into something more, then great. If not, then that's fine too.

Or maybe reading this book has ignited a spark in you that will never be extinguished. You are all in!

Whether or not you see servicing pianos as a calling or as a fulfilling hobby, I strongly recommend joining the Piano Technicians Guild (PTG). There are local chapters throughout North America. Even if you live outside this area, I believe it is still worth joining.

Membership grants you access to over 100 years' worth of technical articles, many of which are stored in a searchable index. You also get access to dozens of hours of online educational video content.

Attend a convention if you can. Imagine spending four days surrounded by hundreds of like-minded piano nerds, participating in classes, concerts, and events. Visit www.ptg.org to find information about how you can join.

PTG also offers the exams required to become a Registered Piano Technician (RPT). You'll notice that this book does not come with a certificate of completion. Instead, I would invite you to use the experience you gained from this book to start you on a journey toward becoming an RPT.

If you live outside of North America, then you should also look up how to get involved in a commensurate professional organization in your area, if one exists. Piano tuning and servicing can be solitary work. There is power in gathering and learning from others.

What else can you do? Well, if you are serious, then the best opportunities available in the United States are the programs at the North Bennet Street School (NBSS) in Boston. They offer a one-year program that covers the basics, and an optional second year program that covers rebuilding. Imagine learning how to work on pianos all day every day from some of the best mentors in the world. Now that is an education worth investing in. Mind you, it is an investment. The program isn't cheap, and neither is living in Boston. That said, graduates from North Bennet are in high demand in our industry. If you want to make this a career, then NBSS is the fastest route to success.

Of course, there are other opportunities for in-person training available. If you are lucky, then there might even be some in your area. Sadly, formal in-person training is hard to come by these days. Today, most people are introduced to this field through an online correspondence course.

There are a handful of nice online courses out there. Personally, I have worked with the Piano Technician Academy (PTA). Their program includes text, images, and professional-level video content that lays out everything we have covered in this book and so much more (including aural tuning skills, basic voicing techniques, more involved piano repairs, and a more in-depth look at building and running a business). I've also designed a number of field service courses, which are also available through PTA for more experienced technicians.

Whichever path you choose, I wish you the best!

There are around 40,000 professional concerts in the United States each year, more than 100 per day. There are also over 13,500 piano teachers. If these piano studios held only one recital per year, then that would be an additional thirty-five piano recitals every day. Add to that the nearly 2,000 colleges and universities offering degrees in music, each boasting 100s of recitals and concerts each year.

I want you to imagine every single one of these performances. Some are taking place in a sold-out concert hall. Others are attended by family and friends in an intimate recital hall on a college campus. While children perform in living rooms or local piano dealerships around the nation.

Now stop and imagine everyone playing the piano at this very moment, in practice rooms and in their homes. Each and every one of them needs a piano technician to enrich their musical pursuits.

At this very moment there is a piano technician in Manhattan boarding the subway with their tool bag. In Montana there is a technician driving hours across vast stretches of highway to service the pianos in small rural towns. In California there is a piano technician sitting in on a recording session touching up the tuning between takes. In Washington DC there is a piano tuner going through security checkpoints to tune at the White House. And in every city at this very moment, there are piano tuners entering countless schools, churches, and homes.

You could be one of them.

Finishing this book marks the first step on your journey.

Now is the time to take the next step!

Appendix 1

A Beginner's Toolkit

Cleaning

- Black paint marker
- Can of compressed air
- Microfiber cloths
- Paintbrush
- Portable vacuum
- Screwdriver (flathead and Phillips)
- Soundboard cleaners
- Windex

Tuning

- Felt mute
- Papp's mute (optional)
- Rubber mute with handle
- Temperament strip (also called a strip mute)
- Tuning device, or piano tuning app
- Tuning lever (not a gooseneck lever)

Upright Regulation

- 8-inch tweezers
- Balance rail punchings
- Capstan regulator
- Combination handle
- Front rail punchings
- Let-off regulator
- Millimeter ruler with slide
- Screwdrivers (flathead and Phillips)
- Small pieces of felt
- Square capstan screw wrench

Grand Regulation

- 8-inch tweezers*
- Balance rail punchings*
- Capstan regulator*
- Drop screwdriver
- Front rail punchings*
- Grand let-off regulating screwdriver
- Millimeter ruler with slide*
- Regulating screwdriver
- Screwdrivers (flathead and Phillips)*
- Spring tool

*Indicates tools also used for upright regulation.

Voicing for Evenness

- Chopstick needle tool
- Upright voicing tool

Basic Repairs

- Brass wire brush
- Crescent wrench (×2)
- Combination handle
- Elmer's glue
- Flange screwdrivers (flathead and Phillips)
- Grand hammer head extractor
- Hypo oiler with a long needle
- Key easing pliers
- Magnetic retrieval tool
- Protek CLP
- Screwdriver (flathead and Phillips)
- Spare felt pieces
- Upright hammer head extractor

String Replacement

- Brass rod
- Coil lifter
- Coil maker
- Dummy tuning pin
- Flat-nose pliers
- Hammer
- Micrometer
- Music wire cutters
- Needle-nose pliers
- Screwdriver
- String (various sizes)
- String hook
- Tuning lever
- Tuning pin crank

Appendix 2

Terminology to Remember

General Terminology

USA	UK (differences in bold)
Action stack	Action stack
Bottom board, or kneeboard	**Bottom door**
Cheekblock	Cheekblock
Damper	Damper
Fall board, key cover, or nameboard	**The fall**
Hammer	Hammer
Key	Key
Keyslip	Keyslip
Key stop rail	Key stop rail
Lid	**Top**
Practice pedal rod	**Celeste rail**
Sostenuto monkey	Sostenuto monkey
Top board	**Top door**
Wippen	**Lever**

Upright Regulation Terminology

USA	UK (differences in bold)
Aftertouch	Aftertouch
Aftertouch gap	Aftertouch gap
Backcheck	**Check**
Balance rail punchings	**Balance rail washers**
Blow distance	**Blow**
Capstan	Capstan

USA	UK (differences in bold)
Catcher	**Balance hammer**
Checking	Checking
Damper	Damper
Damper spoon	Damper spoon
Front rail punchings	**Touch rail washers**
Hammer	Hammer
Hammer butt	Hammer butt
Hammer rest rail	Hammer rest rail
Jack	Jack
Jack toe, or jack tender	Jack toe, or jack tender
Key	Key
Key dip	Key dip
Key height	Key height
Let-off	**Set off**
Let-off button	**Set-off button**
Lost motion	**Waste touch**
Wippen	**Lever**

Grand Regulation Terminology

USA	UK (differences in bold)
Aftertouch	Aftertouch
Aftertouch gap	Aftertouch gap
Aftertouch rise	Aftertouch rise
Backcheck	**Check**
Balance rail punchings	**Balance rail washers**
Blow distance	**Blow**
Capstan	Capstan
Checking	Checking
Damper	Damper
Drop	Drop

USA	UK (differences in bold)
Drop screw	Drop screw
Front rail punchings	**Touch rail washers**
Hammer	Hammer
Hammer knuckle	**Roller**
Jack	Jack
Jack position	Jack position
Jack toe, or jack tender	Jack toe, or jack tender
Key	Key
Key dip	Key dip
Key height	Key height
Let-off	**Set off**
Let-off button	**Set-off button**
Repetition lever	Repetition lever
Repetition lever height	Repetition lever height
Spring tension	Spring tension
Wippen	**Lever**

String Replacement Terminology

USA	UK (differences in bold)
Agraffe	Agraffe
Aliquot	Aliquot
Becket	Becket
Bridge pins	Bridge pins
Hitch pin	Hitch pin
Tuning pin	**Wrest pin**
V-bar, capo bar, or pressure bar	V-bar, capo bar, or pressure bar

Appendix 3

Regulation Specifications

Upright Regulation Points

Regulation Point	Acceptable Range	Adjustment Location	How to Adjust
Natural key height	~65 mm	Balance rail punchings	Add punchings to increase Remove punchings to decrease
Sharp key height	12–13 mm above the naturals	Balance rail punchings	Add punchings to increase Remove punchings to decrease
Natural key dip	~10 mm	Front rail punchings	Add punchings to decrease Remove punchings to increase
Sharp key dip	Set to aftertouch	Front rail punchings	Add punchings to decrease Remove punchings to increase
Lost motion	A small amount before the hammer is engaged	Capstan	Turn counterclockwise to raise the jack Turn clockwise to lower the jack
Blow distance	45 mm ± 2 mm	Hammer rest rail	Add felts underneath to decrease Remove felts underneath to increase
Let-off	2 mm	Let-off button	Turn counterclockwise to decrease Turn clockwise to increase
Checking	12–16 mm	Backcheck	Bend toward the hammer to decrease Bend away from the hammer to increase
Upright aftertouch	A small gap between the top of the jack and the hammer butt (when the hammer is in check)	Blow distance and key dip	Decrease blow distance to increase aftertouch Increase blow distance to decrease aftertouch (Be sure to address lost motion and checking) Increase key dip to increase aftertouch Decrease key dip to decrease aftertouch (Be sure to address checking)

Grand Regulation Points

Regulation Point	Acceptable Range	Adjustment Location	How to Adjust
Natural key height	~60 mm	Balance rail punchings	Add punchings to increase Remove punchings to decrease
Sharp key height	12–13 mm above the naturals	Balance rail punchings	Add punchings to increase Remove punchings to decrease
Natural key dip	~10 mm	Front rail punchings	Add punchings to decrease Remove punchings to increase
Sharp key dip	Set to aftertouch	Front rail punchings	Add punchings to decrease Remove punchings to increase
Jack position	The back of the jack should be aligned with the back of the knuckle core	The jack regulating screw	Turn the screw clockwise to move the jack closer to the player. Turn the screw counterclockwise to move the jack away from the player.
Repetition lever height	The repetition lever should be just high enough to allow the jack to return freely	The repetition lever regulating screw	Turn the screw clockwise to lower the repetition lever. Turn the screw counterclockwise to raise the repetition lever.
Spring tension	From check, when the key is lifted slightly, the hammer should rise completely without a bobble at the top	The repetition spring	Bend the spring up to strengthen Bend the spring down to weaken
Blow distance	46 mm ± 2 mm	Capstan	Turn clockwise to increase Turn counterclockwise to decrease
Let-off	2 mm	Let-off button	Turn counterclockwise to decrease Turn clockwise to increase
Drop	3–4 mm	Drop screw	Turn clockwise to increase Turn counterclockwise to decrease
Checking	12–16 mm	Backcheck	Bend toward the player to decrease Bend away from the player to increase
Grand aftertouch	A small amount of aftertouch rise in the hammer after drop	Blow distance and key dip	Decrease blow distance to increase aftertouch Increase blow distance to decrease aftertouch Increase key dip to increase aftertouch Decrease key dip to decrease aftertouch

Appendix 4

Answer Key

Unit 1 Exam

1. False
2. True
3. Spinet, console, studio, upright grand
4. False
5. False
6. B
7. D
8. A
9. D
10. C and D
11. D
12. False
13. True
14. C
15. A
16. True
17. B
18. True
19. True
20. False

Lesson 8 Quiz

Easy

1. Left
2. Right
3. Left
4. Right
5. Left

Medium

1. Left
2. Left
3. Right
4. Right
5. Right

Hard

1. Left
2. Left
3. Right
4. Right
5. Left

Unit 3 Exam

1. B
2. A
3. C
4. A and D
5. C
6. Key dip – Front rail punchings
   Key height – Balance rail punchings
   Lost motion – Capstan

Let-off – Let-off button

Checking – Backcheck

Blow Distance – Hammer rest rail

7 False

8 A

9 D

10 True

Unit 4 Exam

1 C

2 B

3 A

4 1: The hammer rises from its at-rest position, 2: Let-off, 3:

Drop, 4: Aftertouch rise

5 B

6 Jack position, repetition lever height, and spring tension

7 Blow distance, let-off, drop, and checking

8 Key dip – Front rail punchings

Key height – Balance rail punchings

Jack position – Jack regulating screw

Let-off – Let-off button

Drop – Drop screw

Blow distance – Capstan

Repetition lever height – Repetition lever height screw

Spring tension – Repetition spring

Checking – Backcheck

9 False

10 A and D

Final Exam

1 Spinet, console, studio, upright grand

2 True

3 D

4 False

5 False

6 C

7 A

8 C

9 C

10 A

11 B

12 False

13 D

14 B

15 A and D

16 B

17 A

18 C

19 A

20 C

21 A

22 D

23 True

24 False

25 False

26 True

27 A

28 B

29 1: The hammer rises from its at-rest position, 2: Let-off,

3: Drop, 4: Aftertouch rise

30 Jack position, repetition lever height, and spring tension
31 C
32 A and D
33 False
34 False
35 True
36 False
37 1: Click up, 2: Nudge down, 3: Refine with the z-axis, 4: Test for stability
38 True
39 True
40 B
41 False
42 C
43 B
44 A
45 True
46 B and C
47 C
48 D
49 False
50 False

Index

action, removing upright 11–13
    returning upright 14–15
    removing grand 23–24
    returning grand 26–27
action stack 25–26
aftertouch, grand 109–111
    upright 79–83, 139–140
agraffe 146–149

baby grand 16
backcheck 68–69, 77–78, 93, 105
balance rail 71, 108, 135
    shimming 139–140
bass, tuning 59
beating 39–40
    false 65
becket 146–149
bichords 57
blow distance, grand 102–103, 109–111
    upright 75–76, 80–83
bottom board 9
bridge pins 146–149
broken string 146–149
butt. See hammer butt
buzzing 133–134

capstan 67–68, 72–74, 91–92, 102–103
case parts, removing grand 17–21
    removing upright 7–10
catcher 68–69, 77–78
cents 55, 62–63
center pins 142–143
checking, grand 105–106
    upright 77–78
cheekblocks 18–22, 141–142
clicks 130–132
CLP, Protek. See Protek CLP.
coil 146–149
console upright 6

damper 67–69, 91–93, 144–145
damper spoon 68
dip. See key dip.
drop action 5–6

drop 105–106, 109
dummy pin 146–149

easing a key 141–143
escapement 68, 76–77, 92–93, 104, 109

fallboard 9–10, 19–22
false beats 61
flange screwdriver 130–131
front rail; 71–72, 108–109, 141–143

hammer 67–69, 92–94
hammer butt 72–74, 79–83
hammer knuckle 92, 95–101
hammer rest rail 72–77, 80–83, 102–103, 129–130
hammer shank 110, 130–132
hitch pin 146–149

instability, tuning 57–58

jack 67–69, 72–74, 91–99, 109–110, 143
jack toe 76–77, 103–104

keys 6, 11–12, 25–26, 29, 141–143
keybed 136–137
key dip, grand 108–109
    upright 71–72
key height, grand 108
    upright 70–71
keyslip 17–22, 141–142
knuckle. See hammer knuckle.

leaking dampers 144
let-off, grand 103–104
    upright 76–77
lever, repetition. See repetition lever.
lever, tuning. See tuning lever.
lid 7–8, 17–18
lid prop 7–8, 17–18
loose screw 129–130
lost motion
    upright action 72–74, 139
    pedals 127–128, 145
lyre 138

music desk 5, 17–20
mutes 37–38

nameboard. *See* fallboard.
needling hammers 119–121
North Bennet Street School, 160
note numbers 42

overpull in pitch raising 62–63

pedal 127–128, 136–138
Piano Technician Academy 38, 161
Piano Technicians Guild 2, 160
pin: tuning 43–48, 146–149
    center 142–143
    bridge 146–149
    hitch 146–149
pinblock 45–46
pitch raise 62–63
pressure bar 146–149
Protek CLP 135–137, 146
PTG. *See* Piano Technicians Guild
punchings: balance rail 70–71, 108
    front rail 71–72, 108–109

rattles. *See* buzzing.
Registered Piano Technician 2, 160
repetition lever 95–99

repetition spring 99–101
repinning 143
RPT. *See* Registered Piano Technician.

shank, hammer. *See* hammer shank.
sizes of pianos, grands 16
    uprights 5–6
spinet 5–6
sostenuto monkey 25
spoon, damper. *See* damper spoon.
spring tension 99–101
squeaks 135–138
sticking key 141–143
studio upright 6

top board 8–10
tuning lever 37–38, position 43
tuning pins 43–48, 146–149

unison, beating 40–41, tuning pins 42–44,
    tuning technique 45–58, bass 59, treble
    60–61
upright grand 6

V-bar 146–149
voicing for evenness 119–121

wippen 67–69, 91–92, 95–101

About the Author

Jason Cassel was born and raised in Southern California and now works as a piano technician for the Brigham Young University School of Music in Provo, Utah (an hour south of Salt Lake City). He received his undergraduate degree from BYU in Commercial Music with an emphasis in Sound Recording. While in school, he worked as a student apprentice in the university piano shop.

After graduating and becoming a Registered Piano Technician, Jason moved to Philadelphia to work for the Steinway and Yamaha dealer in that area. After his first son was born, he decided to attend the Masters of Piano Technology program at Florida State University, the only program of its kind in the country, accepting only two graduate students every two years. He spent the summer between semesters as a senior piano technician for the prestigious Aspen Music Festival & School in Colorado.

He has received the Crowl-Travis Member of Note Award for his contributions to the piano industry, as well as the Jack Greenfield Award in recognition of his nearly three dozen articles in the *Piano Technicians Journal*. Additional publications include an ebook on harpsichord maintenance published by Piano Technician Tutorials, and six instructional video courses on aural tuning available through www.onpitch.com.

Jason is a sought-after instructor at conventions for the Piano Technicians Guild and has presented for Piano Technician's Masterclasses, the North Bennet Street School, the Professional Piano Technicians Network, the Music Teachers National Association, the Piano Technology School in the United Kingdom, the New Zealand Piano Tuners and Technicians Guild, and the Australasian Piano Tuners and Technicians Association. He is also a featured instructor for the Piano Technician Academy.

Jason serves as both a Technical and Tuning Examiner for the Piano Technicians Guild and has received manufacturer training from Steinway & Sons, Yamaha, Mason & Hamlin, and Renner USA.

Outside of piano work, Jason enjoys hiking, family bike rides, and playing with his kids. He also loves exploring America's national parks and has a goal to visit them all! Jason lived in Brazil for two years as a missionary helping people overcome addictions, strengthen their marriages, and find hope amidst uncertainty and despair. Ele fala Português! He also spent a semester studying the Old and New Testament in the Holy Land.

Jason lives in Utah with his wife and their two sons.

Image of the author in front of the Renner Exhibit at the Musical Instrument Museum (MIM) in Phoenix, Arizona. A bucket-list worthy destination for any music lover.